Willie Boy & The Last Western Manhunt

By Clifford E. Trafzer

© 2020 by Clifford E. Trafzer

COPYRIGHT NOTICE: The text and images in this book are protected under copyright laws and may not be used in any way without the written permission of the author.

Published by Coyote Hill Press, Camano Island, WA
Layout & Design by Robin S. Hanks

First Edition, 2020
Printed in the United States
ISBN: 978-1-7358615-0-0   All rights reserved.

Research for this volume was made possible from funds provided by the Rupert Costo Endowment for American Indian Affairs at the University of California, Riverside, and 29 Palms Inn, Oasis of Mara.

Cover Art by Chuck Caplinger, Desert Art Studio, Twentynine Palms, California

Contents

Foreward vii
Preface xi
Introduction xix

Chapter 1
Spirit & Change 1
Chapter 2
William, Willie & Carlota 35
Chapter 3
The Love Affair 55
Chapter 4
Losing Carlota 93
Chapter 5
Gunfight at Ruby Mountain 127
Chapter 6
Inglorious End 147
Chapter 7
Redemption and Retrospective 169
Chapter 8
Chemeheuvi Diaspora and Survival 183
Chapter 9
Jason Momoa's *The Last Manhunt* 205

Bibliography 215

The author respectfully dedicates this volume

To the Family of William Mike

To Jason Momoa who had the vision to create The Last Manhunt and seek the advice and permission of Chemehuevi people

To Heidi Grunt, Pat Flanagan, Paul and Jane Smith of the 29 Palms Inn for protecting and preserving a sacred site

Foreword

The saga of Willie Boy has survived over one hundred years and the captivating story remains alive today. American Indians throughout Southern California, the American Southwest, and Great Basin remember the story well. People living in Mojave Desert certainly remember Willie Boy, Carlota, and the last western manhunt. We became aware of the story after visiting residents of the Mojave Desert and learned from local folks about Willie Boy killing William Mike, and the cultural survival of the *Nuwuvi* or Chemehuevi people. We found the story compelling because it was truly a Native American story of love, culture, and tradition. The story of Willie Boy and Carlota also resonates with descendants of the settler communities as well as Indian communities.

Once we learned of the story of Carlota and Willie Boy, we realized it was a great opportunity to tell a captivating Native American story through film from the inside out. It didn't need to be told from an outsider's perspective like most movies about indigenous peoples are. We wanted to share the oral accounts of this story as told by the people themselves. So we reached out to Dean and Darrell Mike of the Twenty-Nine Palms Band of Mission Indians, and we learned that they had worked with historian Clifford Trafzer for nearly twenty years. They recommended we contact Dr. T. to provide foundational information that would help us move the script in an authentic direction. In the spring of 2019, we first called Dr. T. to begin preliminary discussions about the historical aspects to be considered in telling the story of Willie Boy, Carlota, William Mike, and Chemehuevi people. We found that he had in-depth knowledge of the cultural and historical past of *Nuwuvi* and Serrano people who had once lived at the Oasis of Mara and immediately asked him to be a consultant on our film, *The Last Manhunt*.

We found Dr. T. eager and enthusiastic to review a preliminary copy of the movie script. At the same time, the leadership of the Twenty-Nine Palms Tribe sent him a copy of the script. He edited and commented on the work, just as he would evaluate a book manuscript. Dr. T. began a series of conversations with us that led to re-writes that fleshed out the original script. This collaboration led to a moving presentation that is not only historically based, but captures the emotions of the people and a nuanced details of the era and location. In September 2019, we started shooting the movie at the Gilman Ranch in Banning where Willie Boy had murdered William Mike nearly 110 years to the day of the accident.

In the following pages, readers will find the historical newspaper representations of Willie Boy being depicted as a scoundrel, murderer, abuser, and savage. Dr. T. uses original sources, including oral interviews shared by Chemehuevi people. As a historical consultant for our film, he was on set and available to advise us on housing, material culture, clothing, and landscapes. His Epilogue found herein offers details about the role played by Salt Song Singers and their leader, Matthew Hanks Leivas. Photographs found in this book include both historical and contemporary pictures, including shots of the singers and central characters in the film. Finally, this volume is a good read with flowing prose and wonderful descriptions of people and places. Dr. T. uses words to take you to the Gilman Ranch, Whitewater River, The Pipes, and expansive Mojave Desert. He has spent much of his life in the deserts and mountains of Arizona and

California working with the indigenous peoples of the region. Through this colorful and dramatic book, he invites readers into the Chemehuevi world, Mojave Desert, and the lives of Carlota and Willie Boy who will forever be associated with the last western manhunt.

Thomas Pa'a Sibbett and Jason Momoa.

Thomas Sibbett, a Native Hawai'ian, wrote the screenplay for *The Last Manhunt* based on information he learned from his research, visits to important locations, and interviews with Chemehuevi scholars and elders. He is pictured here on the Agua Caliente Indian Reservation near Palm Springs, California. Author's Photograph with permission of Thomas Sibbett.

James Dean Mike and Darrell James Mike played roles in the movie, *The Last Manhunt*. Between filming takes, Jason Momoa and the two boys posed for a photographs on the set in Palm Canyon on the Agua Caliente Indian Reservation. Author's Photograph with the permission of Jason Momoa and Darrell Mike.

Preface

As every writer knows, the inspiration for putting pen to paper varies from book to book and comes from countless sources. After thirty years studying Southern California Indians – including the intriguing story of Willie Boy, Carlota, and the cultural clash surrounding the tumultuous events a century ago – I hardly expected the events leading to this publication. But I couldn't be happier about it.

It was in early spring of 2019 when I first heard from Jason Momoa. He telephoned to learn more about historical accounts surrounding Willie Boy, a Chemehuevi runner who murdered William Mike, the leader of the Twenty-Nine Palms Band of Mission Indians. Momoa had heard about Willie Boy from residents living in the Mojave Desert. Intrigued by the story, Momoa reached out to members of the modern Twenty-Nine Palms Tribe, who shared some accounts of William Mike, his daughter, Carlota, and Willie Boy. In turn, the Tribe referred Momoa to me for a historical background on the Chemehuevi people and the historical facts surrounding the tale of Willie Boy, Carlota, and the Southern California white establishment.

During our initial conversations, Momoa's interest in getting the factual elements right was quickly evident, as he listened carefully and asked informed questions. It came as no surprise, then, when I learned of his interest in making a full-length motion picture based on the Willie Boy affair of 1909, including the manhunt carried out by lawmen from Riverside and San Bernardino Counties of Southern California. Soon I was conferring with Thomas Sibbett, the screenwriter for the upcoming movie version of the Willie Boy story, *The Last Manhunt*. As Momoa and The Pride of

Gypsies Production Company planned to begin shooting the movie in the first and last parts of summer and early fall of 2019, I joined the production as an historical and cultural consultant with *Nuwuvi* elders, especially my longtime friend, Chemehuevi elder Matthew Hanks Leivas of the Chemehuevi Tribe.

In 2015's *A Chemehuevi Song: Resiliency of a Southern Paiute Tribe*, I included the tribal tragedy associated with Willie Boy, William Mike, and Carlota Mike. Spurred by my conversations with Jason Momoa, this present account details the Native American story about Willie Boy, using information and interpretations I gained through oral interviews with Chemehuevi, Southern Paiute, and Quechan individuals. Their version of the Willie Boy affair focused on cultural causations and consequences; a very unsettling story. While oral history makes up a critical part of research for this study, I've also accessed key documents, newspapers, reports, and secondary literature. Several sources are referenced in the text, but without footnoting those sources are to provide greater continuity for readers. Oral histories recorded by others, offering Native American testimony recorded by Maude Russell, James Sandos, Larry Burgess, and me, further provide depth to understanding of the events leading to the tragedy of Willie Boy. Over the course of many years, various tribal elders have shared their knowledge with me, particularly Dean Mike, Darrell Mike, Joe Mike Benitez, Jennifer Mike, Larry Eddy, Matt Leivas, Robert Chavez, Kenneth Anderson, Alfreda Mitre, Dorothy Mathews, and other Native individuals who wished to remain anonymous. Many people gave me their time and knowledge, including Paul and Jane Smith of the 29 Palms Inn in the town of Twentynine Palms, where they watch over and protect the old site of the Chemehuevi and Serrano village at the Oasis of Mara.

Since my childhood in Yuma, Arizona, stories about an elusive character named Willie Boy intrigued me. During my research in the 1990s into the history of the Twenty-Nine Palms Tribe, tribal stories about Willie Boy, the murder of William Mike, and the last western manhunt formed a recurring subject of discussion. Tribal elders from throughout the region – Quechan, Mojave from Fort Mojave and Mohave from the Colorado River Indian Tribes, Cahuilla, Kumeyaay, Southern Paiute, Chemehuevi – had learned about Willie Boy from family elders, people with first-hand knowledge of Willie Boy. "You know, don't you," they'd tell me, "that Willie Boy got away." And while the conventional western interpretation paints Willie Boy as a violent criminal, there is a distinctly different perception: Willie Boy is a heroic character who outsmarted and out-ran the lawmen pursuing him. And in an era when the law was too often stacked against Native Americans in favor of white law enforcement, Willie Boy symbolized successful resistance to arrest, imprisonment, and hanging by county sheriffs. Outlaw Willie Boy eluded sheriffs and settlers eager to capture and kill him.

But for decades the telling of Willie Boy's story has been dominated by journalists, entertainers, and law enforcement individuals. Since 1909, theatrical plays have caricatured Willie Boy, culminating in a full-length motion picture about the Chemehuevi runner. In Morongo Valley, entrepreneurs opened Willie Boy's Saloon and Barbeque on the trail that Willie Boy and Carlota used on their escape from Banning, California. Invariably these two-dimensional depictions presented Willie Boy from the perspective of western-oriented institutions, without the nuance provided when studying the Native American element. Native or white, many people view Willie Boy as a villain whose actions led to the deaths of Mr. Mike and Carlota. Certainly members of the Mike family do not perceive Willie Boy to be a heroic figure. His actions led to William Mike's murder, the leader of the Twenty-Nine Palms Band of Chemehuevi and patriarch of the extended Mike family. Regardless, most Chemehuevi and other *Nuwuvi* people believe that Willie Boy eluded the posse after the gunfight at Ruby Mountain, living out his life in Southern Nevada among Southern Paiute people. Willie Boy, they say, died of tuberculosis years after the tragic events. No one has revealed his burial site, which adds to the mystery of Willie Boy.

The divergence in the stories told about Willie Boy, especially concerning actions following the death of William Mike, are rooted in cultural disparities. The Chemehuevi story surrounding the Willie Boy affair differs greatly from that of the posse. Indian accounts center on issues inherent in Native culture, especially tribal marriage laws. To fully understand what occurred, those cultural issues must be appreciated. According to ancient tribal law, contemporary Indian elders explain that Willie Boy and Carlota were cousins and too closely related to marry. Both Carlota's and Willie Boy's families objected to their union, but these were young people living in a new age that defied strict adherence to the old laws. When Willie Boy and Carlota opted to "go against the song of creation" and marry, events unfolded leading to the death of three people—William and Carlota Mike as well as Willie's grandmother, Mrs. Ticup. Tribal elders have shared Willie Boy stories for over one hundred years. Those stories have largely been ignored by historians as inaccurate and biased, while accounts in newspapers and testimony of posse members and law enforcement are accepted as verified truth, though these sources had much to gain from lying. Are those outside the Native community correct when they say there's no truth in accounts given by Native Americans? No living person knows the actual truth of what happened. But looking at both sets of reporting – Native and white – is instructive. In this text, I offer an interpretation based on Native American testimony, some understanding of Chemehuevi culture, and my scholarly work with the Mike family and other *Nuwuvi* people.

Tribal elders have been my teachers. For that reason, I am deeply indebted to members of the Mike family, the Twenty-Nine Palms Band of Mission Indians, and Chemehuevi people living near Havasu Landing, California, and Parker, Arizona. I wish to thank Chairman Darrell Mike, Dean Mike, Jennifer Mike, Joe Mike Benitez, Larry Eddy, and Betty Cornelius. The Hanks Leivas family has been especially kind to me, sharing their knowledge, culture, and landscape. I thank the Hanks Leivas family, especially Gertrude, Matthew, Mary, June, Juliana, Hope, Danny, and Iris. In addition, Vivienne Jake helped me understand *Nuwuvi* beliefs about power, song, ceremony, and family in understanding the culture of the people. They graciously volunteered their knowledge and helped me learn and understand the indigenous interpretation of the Willie Boy affair and western manhunt. I thank members of the Twenty-Nine Palms Band of Mission Indians for their support of this project and friendship of many years. I thank Heidi Grunt, Pat Flanagan, Paul and Jane Smith of the 29 Palms Inn for sharing their knowledge of the Oasis of Mara and for preserving the sacred site of the former village of Chemehuevi and Serrano people. The 29

Palms Inn sits on the grounds of the former Indian village, and the proprietors of the Inn preserve and protect the old village site from development. People associated with the 29 Palms Inn supported the creation of this book, which helped me conduct research at the Oasis of Mara, Old School House Archives, and Twentynine Palms City Library.

Talented artist, Chuck Caplinger of the Desert Art Studio provided the cover art for this book, using the only known photograph of Willie Boy to represent the Chemehuevi runner. Unfortunately, no known photograph of Carlota exists. The painting on the cover of Carlota and Willie Boy is an artist rendition of the couple and not based on a photograph of the couple. I am indebted to Chuck and Holgie for their hospitality when I visited the studio to work on the cover art. I also thank Cheryl Cox, Daisy Ocampo, Pat Flanagan and Henry Vasquez who read drafts of my manuscript and offered criticisms. My colleagues at the University of California have supported and encouraged my research for many years, especially Kim Wilcox, Josh Gonzales, Amanda Wixon, Andrew Shaler, Monte Kugel, and my graduate students. Karen Raines and Cherry Williams of Special Collections in the Rivera Library went out of their way to help me research and acquire photographs for this book. Raines also helped me locate newspapers about the last western manhunt, which reveal as much about yellow journalism to sell newspapers as they do about historical events associated with Willie Boy.

James Sandos and Larry Burgess have been friends and colleagues for many years. They have supported my work and advanced this study through the oral histories they recorded in the 1990s with Chemehuevi elders from the families of Willie Boy and William Mike. Tribal elders trusted

Jim and Larry. They gradually shared their family accounts, saying they wished to correct the record left by members of the posse, newspaper reporters, and past writers. Southern Paiute and Chemehuevi elders enriched my study by offering their testimony, including Matthew Hanks Leivas, Alfreda Mitre, Kenneth Anderson, Dorothy Mathews, Bonita Eddy Fernandez, Robert Chavez, Iris Burns Leivas, and *Nuwuvi* individuals who wished to remain anonymous. Salt Song and Ghost Dance singers not previously mentioned included: Daniel Leivas, Joseph Jimenez, Brian Kellywood, Isaac Ochoa, Matthew Cruz, Jaymeee Moore, Susan Nez, Maryam Salazar, Darren Spivey, John Smith, Nogwa Smith, Aya Smith, and Alex Espinosa. I thank the Cahuilla Bird Singers and Salt Song Singers for sharing the Willie Boy Song, especially my friend, Luke Madrigal, who walked on during the production of this book. As part of *The Last Manhunt*, Matthew Leivas and singers from the Chemehuevi and Colorado River Indian Reservations sang Salt Songs and a *Nuwuvi* Ghost Dance Song to add credibility to the film.

I owe a debt of gratitude to Jason Momoa, Christian Camargo, Thomas Sibbett, Eric Laciste, Maluhia Kinimaka, Dan Clifton, Martin Kistler, Michele Cicero, and Brian Mendoza for their commitment to present historical events and people sensitively. All the participants involved in the filming of *The Last Manhunt* provided me a better understanding of film making. I enjoyed being a part of movie making and contributing to its authenticity, which actor Jason Momoa, screenwriter Thomas Sibbett, and director Christian Camargo sought to achieve. Actors, artists, and producers attempted to present the movie in an historical context and accurately represent the period and people. I was honored to serve as an historical consultant during the summer 2019 and particularly enjoyed watching select scenes, especially the filming of the Ghost Dance. Furthermore, I was pleased that tribal members Angelina Mike and her two sons, Xol Antonius Nunez-Mike and Cruz Guillaume-Nunez Mike, as well as two sons of Darrell and Corina Mike, James Dean Mike and Darrell James Mike II, had parts in the movie. Their involvement in the movie, like that of the Chemehuevi singers, brought authenticity to the film that represented Chemehuevi people.

For many years, Richard and Robin Hanks have encouraged me in my research, and we enjoyed a few evenings visiting about book projects. I express my deep gratitude for their interest in the Willie Boy book. After going through the review process, they both agreed to publish the present work through Coyote Hill Press. It is an honor for me to have Coyote Hill Press publish the work and for Robin and Richard to design and produce *Willie Boy & The Last Western Manhunt*. I thank my family and friends for their support. Lee Ann revised the manuscript and skillfully produced the final version. Richard Hanks copyedited the manuscript, and my daughter, Tess, cleaned up the photographs. Hayley, Tara, Tess, Jeff, Travis, and Louise lent moral support. Sisters Sally and Donna encouraged the writing project. I thank everyone involved in the creation of this work, particularly *Nuwuvi* families that shared their knowledge and interpretations.

Clifford E. Trafzer
Yucaipa, California
August 2020

Introduction

Willie Boy's life is shrouded in mystery, half-truths, and outright lies. Not much is known generally about Willie Boy and his life before 1909, except that his mother, Mary Snyder, gave birth to her son in an adobe house located in Chemehuevi Valley near the banks of the Colorado River. Willie Boy was born into *Nuwuvi* people, the remarkable Southern Paiute people of the Great Basin, Southwest, and Southern California. Cahuilla elder Harold Matthews told his second wife, Gabrieleño Band of Mission Indians elder Dorothy Matthews, that Harold's first wife was Clarice Bow. Clarice was a woman of Southern Paiute blood but enrolled on the Agua Caliente Indian Reservations. Clarice claimed Willie Boy's last name was Bow, changed by those that heard his name as Boy rather than Bow. She also said that Willie Boy was born on the Moapa Indian Reservation, but this has not been verified. *Nuwuvi* people from the Colorado River say he was born at Chemehuevi Valley. In any case, as a young man, Willie Boy ventured out from *Nuwuvi* communities to work as a cowboy on ranches.

A white rancher reportedly taught Willie Boy how to shoot a gun, and Willie Boy became an exceptional shot with a rifle. Willie Boy became an amazing athlete and runner and because of this the society of Chemehuevi runners invited him into their small cadre of accomplished athletes. They taught Willie Boy to "run in the old way" or as elder Joe Mike Benitez explained, run in "the magical way." Chemehuevi and other *Nuwuvi* people believe that Willie Boy and the other special *Nuwuvi* runners could teleport—they could fly. As one elder pointed out, he ran like the wind.

A similar mystery surrounds the lives of *puahgaant* or shaman William Mike and his oldest daughter, Carlota. Born in 1844 or 1845, William Mike entered the world at the same time Texas joined the Union and as James K. Polk became the eleventh president of the United States. He preceded the birth of Wovoka, the Ghost Dance Prophet, by more than a decade. Both men followed a powerful spiritual path, but William Mike followed a traditional path as a tribal shaman, rather than becoming a Ghost Dancer. In his youth during the 1860s, William Mike fought in the Mojave-Chemehuevi War as a warrior, ultimately turning to a life as a healer and leader of the Twenty-Nine Palms Band of Chemehuevi. But for all his leadership qualities, William Mike is remembered most notably for the manner of his demise. William Mike was shot and killed by a young Chemehuevi man named Willie Boy.

The personal lives of settlers found in this account likewise remains scant. Their greatest contribution historically developed after the death of William Mike, when the western manhunt ensued in the fall of 1909. Numerous white posse members and a few Indian trackers participated in the manhunt. Their names appear briefly in newspaper accounts and government reports about the manhunt and its aftermath. Willie Boy is best known for his exploits against the posse as they tracked him. And it's here the accounts diverge: the lawmen claim they found Willie Boy dead after he murdered Carlota in the desert. Native voices claim Willie Boy survived. The oral testimony of Chemehuevi elders, past and present, poses an alternative account of the Willie Boy affair.

For many years, Native Americans kept their own accounts of Willie Boy, Carlota, William Mike, and Mrs. Ticup (Willie Boy's grandmother), passing them down through oral histories passed through the years by tribal elders. They shared their stories about Willie Boy with each other and with their children, though sparingly. Speaking of the dead constituted a cultural infraction that could, in Chemehuevi beliefs, harm members of their families. Chemehuevi elder Joe Mike Benitez, the grandson of William Mike, explained that *Nuwuvi* cultural law prevented people from speaking much about the dead or even uttering their names. To do so risked bringing illness or death to those violating tribal laws. Joe explained that his uncles refused to utter a word about Willie Boy. Traditional law forbade his family from speaking of Willie Boy, and the trauma of losing their father and sister through violence weighed heavily on them.

Joe's mother, Susie Mike, ultimately shared some stories about Willie Boy, Carlota, and William Mike. Significantly, in the 1980s and 1990s, a few more Chemehuevi elders shared their oral histories about Willie Boy with historians James Sandos and Larry Burgess. These two remarkable scholars successfully worked with Chemehuevi elders living on the Cabazon and Colorado River Indian Reservations and tribal elders agreed to tell Burgess and Sandos details that they had never shared before with people outside their families. Sandos and Burgess gathered the first comprehensive oral histories about Willie Boy, Carlota, and William Mike, which have been invaluable in the present work. Their extensive research led to the publication of their landmark book, *The Hunt for Willie Boy*. After decades of non-Native control over the story, Chemehuevi tribal elders and members of the families of Willie Boy and William Mike agreed that the time had come for them to speak of Willie Boy, to share their coveted knowledge with two researchers they trusted.

In the words of Chief Yellow Wolf, "Nobody to help us tell our side—the whites told only one side. Told it to please themselves." *Nuwuvi* people felt past writers and a movie project portrayed the posse's stories, not that of Chemehuevi Indians. Following the ancient tradition of not speaking at length about past relatives who have walked on into the Milky Way, contemporary descendants of the Mike family have little to say about their ancestors, William and Carlota Mike. And even today, talking about the death of William Mike and Carlota causes trauma among contemporary Mike family members. A small portion of what is known and kindly shared by a few family members appears in the following pages.

I present *Willie Boy: The Last Western Manhunt* with the deepest respect for the extended family of William Mike as well as other *Nuwuvi* people who gifted me with indigenous knowledge they wished to share. This was not an easy avenue – the people and events involved in the Willie Boy saga constitute a tragedy for many Chemehuevi and Southern Paiute. The story involves the violation of a highly significant cultural norm of the *Nuwuvi*: incest, or marriage within a certain degree of kinship. And to understand the fundamental nature of this issue in the Willie Boy story, we need to consider the cultural value system of the *Nuwuvi*. Across time and distance, civilizations establish codes of behavior that govern a particular society. Consider the Judeo-Christian traditions established in the first books of the Bible. Native Americans are no different. At the beginning of time, *Nuwuvi* Creators had given the Chemehuevi and Southern Paiute laws by which to live and those born into the culture were expected to follow the laws or cultural rules of their ancestors. Elders conveyed ancestral teachings and cultural norms through song and stories and all young people, including Willie Boy and Carlota, were expected to adhere to ancestral teachings of their elders. So, when Willie Boy and Carlota fell in love and wished to marry, they did so despite knowing they were too closely related, most likely first cousins, well within the prohibited degree of kinship. Having been born into the culture of *Nuwuvi* people, Willie Boy and Carlota knew the correct behavior expected of them.

During the late nineteenth and early twentieth centuries, white settlers of Southern California, Southern Nevada, and Northern Arizona knew little or nothing of *Nuwuvi* culture. Worse yet, most settlers cared little or nothing about the "primitive" ways of Southern Paiute people, often casting the people as "diggers," a pejorative way of calling *Nuwuvi* people the N word. Many settlers denigrated the Southern Paiute and their cultures, claiming the people had no religion, government, laws, economies, or morals. Settlers sometimes claimed Chemehuevi people to be more related to animals than humans, portraying them as shiftless beings moving about each day with no purpose other than to feed themselves, hand to mouth. Although this was not true, the image affected the way newspaper reporters and writers presented Southern Paiute and Chemehuevi in the written word. Writers without knowledge of *Nuwuvi* people presented their works as if they were factual. A gullible, uninformed public accepted false information and interpretations that harmed the public's way of thinking and knowing about Willie Boy, Carlota, William Mike, and *Nuwuvi* people generally.

Willie Boy and Carlota grew up during a difficult era of American History when white settlement greatly impacted the lives of Native Americans everywhere, especially the

American West. Spanish and Mexican exploration minimally touched Chemehuevi people—the southern-most group of *Nuwuvi* people. However, in the aftermath the war between the United States and Mexico, American trappers, traders, explorers, soldiers, settlers, steamboat operators, missionaries, miners, and others significantly influenced the course of *Nuwuvi* culture and history. Beginning in the 1850s and continuing throughout the late nineteenth and early twentieth centuries, settlers from many backgrounds and professions moved up and down the Colorado River. At the same time, emigrant wagon trains moved west along the 32nd and 35th parallels, crossing the great stream into California. Settlers moved to and through Indian Country, threatening the cultural ways of Chemehuevi, Mojave, Quechan, and many California Indians.

At the same time, the United States influenced American Indian policies and cultures through the Army, Office of Indian Affairs, and acts of Congress. Indians responded to white emigration in many ways. Some fought the government, but others tried accommodation and reconciliation. Either way, Indians saw their lives and cultures changing and feared the old ways would never live again. During the nineteenth century, a new religious movement emerged and spread first among Northern Paiute people that influenced the course of *Nuwuvi* history. Willie Boy became a participant in the Ghost Dance Movement and learned of the teachings of the Paiute Prophet. Born in 1856, Wovoka, the Ghost Dance Prophet, grew up in an earlier Ghost Dance movement of the 1870s. His father and other followers of the first Ghost Dance influenced the new movement that emerged later.

On January 1, 1889, Wovoka had a religious experience that affected the lives of thousands of American Indians living in the American West, including Willie Boy. Wovoka died, visited the Creator, and returned to earth with the Creator's message for all Native Americans to sing and dance at five night intervals. According to Wovoka, participating in the Ghost Dance Ceremony would hasten the Indian apocalypse and the world would be set right again. An apocalypse is generally not something to be eagerly anticipated, but in the Ghost Dance apocalypse the earth would return to its aboriginal state. Native Americans from past generations would return to earth to live in a world filled with game animals, plants, and a pristine environment for Indian people. Wovoka preached peace among all peoples, including settlers, but urged Native American adherents to follow his holy instructions to do no one harm. Ghost Dancers, Wovoka proclaimed, had to keep the faith that the Creator would turn the world over, bring back the ancestors, and return the earth to its original state as an indigenous place. According to the Ghost Dance Prophet, the earth would forever be wholly indigenous again without the influences of white people.

As a young man, Willie Boy joined in Ghost Dancing among the Chemehuevi and Hualapai Indians where he learned the precepts of the prophet Wovoka. Like the other dancers, Willie Boy painted himself with white clay and participated in the Ghost Dance Ceremony of his people. By joining other Ghost Dancers, the Chemehuevi runner sought a new way of being Native through the Ghost Dance. Willie Boy realized that white settlement had brought many irreversible and rapid changes to the Indian world, which his tribal leaders and shaman seemed helpless to stop. White encroachment and influences came fast and furious among

American Indian people. As a young man, Willie Boy grew up in the Chemehuevi culture and language, but he branched out to participate in the Ghost Dance while seeking employment from white ranchers, riding herd on horseback like other cowboys. He learned to shoot firearms and became a superior marksman. At the same time, he avoided the pitfalls of drinking, smoking, and gambling. Employers considered him trustworthy and a good worker. He spoke his own *Nuwuvi* language while also learning English, demonstrating an intelligent, adaptive nature. As a young man he dressed in a dapper fashion, and used his wages to buy a white shirt, sports jacket, laced shoes, stylish hat, and a necktie; unusual dress for most Native Americans of the early twentieth century, especially those too poor to buy manufactured clothing. He used his money to pay a photographer for a studio shot of himself dressed in his sport coat and tie. This photograph offers us the best picture we have of Willie Boy, revealing a pragmatic self-awareness.

Willie Boy seemed to adopt some of the selfish ways of the *Haiko*, the white people. As a child growing up in Chemehuevi Valley, he had learned the value of cooperation, sharing, and caring for others. In settler communities, he learned to be self-centered and individualistic, doing and acting in a manner that he felt was best for himself and not necessarily the group. Perhaps through the Ghost Dance or through his interactions with settlers, Willie Boy began to suppress his indigenous teachings and embrace the code of the rugged individualist, acting in his own interests rather than strictly follow his childhood teachings. As he pivoted away from the Chemehuevi songs of creation and the rules set down at creation for all *Nuwuvi* people to follow,

Willie Boy broke from tradition and headed directly into a confrontation between Native culture and white ways.

Willie Boy's story can be viewed as a hero's journey in this Native telling. His initial choice to follow a negative course brought him pain and suffering of his own making. It took the tragedy of William Mike and Carlota's deaths before he returned to the ways of his people. Having stepped away from his culture and holy beliefs, Willie Boy finally "returned home" to ask shamans to "fix him" or bring him back into balance with his tribal ways. As contemporary Chemehuevi tribal elder Matthew Hanks Leivas has said, "the shamans at Pahrump did the best that they could for Willie Boy, but they could only do so much because of all the bad things he had done."

Willie Boy's pursuit of redemption, his attempt to become culturally whole again, reflects a tragic journey that still resonates today, over a hundred years on from the deaths of William Mike and Carlota. In his journey to survive, Willie Boy challenged numerous lawmen eager to capture or kill him, prompting the posse, press, and citizens to demonize Willie Boy. He was described as "stark mad," a devil, demon, fiend, crazy, and insane. The lawmen claimed Willie Boy had an "unbalanced mind," but the Chemehuevi runner used his cunning, intelligence, and experience to outsmart the posse and survive a dangerous gunfight on Ruby Mountain. Willie Boy lived on for many years, only to face his own demons when his grandmother shamed him for all his wrongdoings. He left the village at Twenty-Nine Palms, located at the present site of the 29 Palms Inn, to run north into the Bullion Mountains. Although he ran from his aunts and grandmother, he could not run from himself and his past or escape the fact that his acts had caused pain, suffering, and death to his family and the family of William Mike. He defeated the posse only to face his real enemy—himself. He ran on to Red Ant Hill near Pahrump, Nevada, where he spoke to his Creator and his sacred mountain, *Nivagaanti*. On the slopes of Red Ant Hill, Willie Boy sought the power of the Spirit to help him find his way.

Chapter 1
Spirit and Change

In the *Tiwiinyarivipi,* that part of the world known to the Chemehuevi Indians as the "storied landscape," *So Iris,* also known as Mary Snyder, brought her son into this world. In 1882, she gave birth to Willie Boy, most likely in the Chemehuevi Valley along the banks of the Colorado River. Willie Boy entered the Chemehuevi world at a turbulent time during an age of transition. The Chemehuevi were the southern-most group of Southern Paiutes living along the Colorado River, and on adjacent lands in the Mojave Desert and the Colorado Desert, within the modern-day borders of California and Arizona. Small villages lay scattered throughout the region. Growing up in the mountains and deserts of eastern California, Willie Boy also spent a good deal of time in Western Arizona. Wherever he lived, he was immersed in the ways and traditions of the *Nuwuvi* people. He traveled both sides of the wild Colorado River before dams obstructed its natural flow. He visited the hot and cold springs dotting the desert landscape on the eastern edge of present-day San Bernardino County. But Willie Boy also experienced the increasing disruption brought to Indian Country by white settlers who occupied Indian lands, altering the lives and traditions of Native people. With the passing of every year, settlers expanded their influence across the greater American Southwest and Great Basin.

Despite the encroachment of white society, Chemehuevi traditions maintained a strong influence. It was the Mojave who gave the name Chemehuevi to the *Nuwuvi* people. And although little evidence exists directly relating to Willie Boy's early life, traditional Chemehuevi life in the early 1900s reflects the type of upbringing Willie Boy experienced. He grew up in a traditional manner, learning first from the prominent women in his life: his mother, his grandmother, and his aunties. With time, the elder men in his family and community would have become a growing influence. Following the Chemehuevi way, Willie played with children he called "brothers" or "sisters" or "cousins," whether or not he was blood related to them. Kinship was highly significant to these tribal people, and close connections were often equated with blood relationships.

    Willie Boy's childhood home was a one-room rectangular structure known as a *samarókwai*, a rather permanent house made of log posts, sticks, and plant material as insulation. The people packed wet adobe on the sides and roof of their lodges, smearing the mud with their hands and leaving the imprints of their fingers on the interior and exterior walls. The seasons determined where the family slept: in winter, Willie Boy and his family slept inside the house; in summer, they slept outside to avoid the burning heat of the sun, often under a brush arbor they called a *takagani* or flat house. Families cooked outside or under a brush lean-to attached to their home. When the people moved out of Chemehuevi Valley to hunt or gather, they build a *tcuupikyani,* a small round house that sat on the ground without wooden supports being driven into the earth. The *tcuupikyani* was made of plant materials thatched together over a wooden frame built in the round, sometimes with willow limbs and branches leaning against a central pole. Up to a quarter of the building might be left open for easy entrance and exit. Smoke from small fires used for light, warmth, and cooking inside the lodge easily escaped from a shelter constructed in the style of the *tcuupikyani*.

What might Willie Boy have experienced during his childhood? In particular, what skills and beliefs and cultural traditions made him the Chemehuevi man he ultimately became? Consider the traditional life of a Chemehuevi, because without understanding that part of this story, the rest will only read from the Euro-American perspective. Traditional Chemehuevi culture was kept alive, generation to generation, by storytelling. During cold winter nights in the desert, parents and grandparents told the children ancient stories, repeating the tales many times over the course of the winter. The repetition was deliberate. Children would hear the stories and be expected to repeat them, until they could recite them word for word. Stories about *Hutsipamamauu*, or Ocean Woman, were central to Chemehuevi cosmology. The most significant female Creator, Ocean Woman existed at a time when water or primordial soup surrounded the entire earth. At the beginning of *Nuwuvi* time, Ocean Woman fell to earth from the sky world, the land above the earth, and became the first of all Creators. Initially she walked on the water's surface, but she was not content with a world only filled with water. She envisioned solid land with mountains, valleys, foothills, lakes, rivers, oceans, caves, plains, and plateaus. She envisioned a world of color, plants, and animals.

With this vision in mind, Ocean Woman set out to create a solid earth. She began by stroking the dry skin on the inside of her upper legs, rolling her hands as she sprinkled the dry bits of skin onto the water. When enough of the debris formed a membrane-like surface, Ocean Woman lay down on the skin and gazed at the sky, gently floating until she reached the center of the earth; the heart of *Nuwuvi* Country.

By stretching out her body, pushing and pulling her legs and arms, hands and head and torso, Ocean Woman twisted and turned as she transformed her body into a gigantic mass of earth, created contours in a great and diverse landscape.

Deep in her imagination, Ocean Woman envisioned her first helpers, beings she called *Cinaavi* (Coyote), *Tukumumuuntsi* (Mountain Lion), and *Tivatsi* (Wolf). These animal people or holy beings helped Ocean Woman create the earth. Ocean Woman continually stretched out her body, forming the massive landscapes and geographical features of North and South America. Listening to these stories, Willie Boy would have learned that the creases in Ocean Woman's body formed fault lines on top of and inside the earth. When Ocean Woman moves today, these faults slip and slide causing earthquakes, evidence that Ocean Woman is alive and continues to change the face of the earth.

Through the oral tradition of Chemehuevi people, Willie Boy learned that periodically, Ocean Woman sent her helpers out from the center of the earth to report on her progress. She labored day and night until Coyote and Cougar reported the earth was completed. The land had length and width. But Ocean Woman continued to shift about and the people felt her move occasionally. Willie Boy's people said Ocean Woman animated the earth, brought it to life with land and water, and remains a central part of the earth today. The Spring Mountains located west of Las Vegas, Nevada, were the origin point for the *Nuwuvi*, with the first beings living on top of the mountains. Wolf and Coyote, for example, lived in massive caves on a great peak known as *Nivagaanti* or Having Snow. Today, the people call it Snow Mountain, an appropriate name since snow sits on the peak much of the year. The highest peak, *Nivagaanti,* is known today as Mount Charleston. It is the foremost—the most important--of all peaks in the *Nuwuvi* world. This magnificent peak stands tall in a massive mountain range surrounded by lesser mountains, deserts, and valleys. Snow Mountain rises 11, 918 feet high. *Nuwuvi* people refer to Snow Mountain as "My Mountain." Spirits live there, including Ocean Woman, the first Creator. As a child, Willie Boy heard stories about *Nivagaanti* and the holy beings that lived and live today on the creation mountain. The mountain is sacred to the people. It is eternal. It calls the clouds for rain and snow, and water flows down from mountain heights as does spiritual power emanating from its heights like a great, invisible spider web.

    Ocean Woman began a process of creation that continued with the making of the first men and women. The Creator took on many forms and functions at the beginning of time. For example, at one point, Ocean Woman transformed herself into a beautiful woman known as *Poowavi* or Louse who jogged about naked except for a *nawi* or an apron, which she wore to conceal her vulva. On one particular occasion Louse began a journey west to see her mother, and as she jogged along, her apron flipped up and down, revealing her vagina. As she moved merrily along, she sang: "My Little Jackrabbit Apron, Flaps Up and Down, Flaps Up and Down!" Coyote was out hunting and spotted *Poowavi's* tracks, following them until he saw this voluptuous woman. Coyote stopped *Poowavi* to express his desire to make love with her. She paused, eyed him coyly, then instructed Coyote to race ahead and build a small round lodge for them to share that night. Coyote followed the directions as quickly as he could, building the little house and waiting inside for Louse to arrive. As Louse approached the lodge, she focused her thoughts on urging Coyote to fall asleep, and he did!

When Coyote awoke, he realized he had slept until morning. Louse had moved on and Coyote hurried to catch her, following the beauty's tracks. Upon catching up with Louse, Coyote was again instructed to hurry along, build a house for them to share that night. Four times this exact scenario occurred, each time Coyote fell asleep and missed his opportunity for lovemaking. By the time Coyote reached Louse after the fourth night, she stood on the shores of the Pacific Ocean and divulged her final plan: to swim to an island in the middle of the ocean and reunite with her mother. Coyote begged to go with her, but he could not swim. Louse – wishing to be rid of her stalker – offered to carry him on her back as she swam out into the open ocean. Once she was far out of sight of the shore, she dove to the bottom of the sea in an attempt to drown Coyote, though he survived … barely. With Coyote off her back, Louse swam to the surface to continue her journey to her mother's island.

Coyote avoided drowning by clawing his way to the surface and transforming into *Pahokosowavi* or Water Spider. He skirted across the surface of the Pacific Ocean and arrived on an island. Exhausted, he resumed his identity as Coyote as he walked into a small settlement. Coyote walked past an older woman weaving a large basket and into a small lodge where he fell fast asleep. Not long after, Louse swam ashore and approached her mother, telling her of the persistent Coyote. Her mother announced that she knew the horny devil, who was asleep in the nearby lodge. With a change of heart, Louse now consented to make love with Coyote, who eagerly agreed. To his dismay, the experience was a challenging one: Louse's vagina was embedded with sharp teeth. Coyote persevered and spent a (mostly) satisfying night with Louse. The following morning, Coyote announced his resolve to return home to *Nivagaanti*. Louse's elder mother handed him a large basket, directing him to take it to his brother, Wolf, who would know what to do with its contents.

The contents of the basket will be surprising to no one except Coyote, who seemed unaware that the basket contained many eggs produced by his union with Louse. With the basket on his back, Coyote returned to the mainland as *Pahokosowavi*, changing into his old self and trotting across the landscape, continually checking behind him to confirm no one was following him. Strange noises coming from the basket puzzled Coyote, who'd been warned to deliver the basket to Wolf unopened. But Coyote's curiosity got the better of him, and he paused long enough to open the basket. Much to his surprise, the first human beings scrambled out of the basket and swiftly ran off in every direction.

The escaping humankind moved off to form their own tribes and cultures, but at the bottom of the basket lay a number of people, crushed by their fellow humans. Coyote sealed the basket and carried his lighter load to his brother's cave at Snow Mountain. By the time he reached *Nivagaanti*, Wolf, the wise one with knowledge and forethought, realized Coyote's rash actions and admonished him for his impulsive disregard for the instructions given him by Louse's elder mother. Wolf opened the basket, bringing forth the lame and crushed humans and tapping his powerful medicine to blow life into them. These reanimated figures became the strongest and most intelligent of all human beings, populating Snow Mountain and dispersing in all directions, forming many diverse bands. Willie Boy knew from the stories that these people were his ancestors, the first *Nuwuvi*, the product of the union of Louse and Coyote.

As a child, Willie Boy absorbed the stories of Ocean Woman, Coyote, Wolf, and Louse. While versions of the stories circulated among all *Nuwuvi* people, the central themes remained the same. These and other stories shaped *Nuwuvi* culture, including those describing *puha* or power that came to earth from the sky world when Ocean Woman first fell to the ocean. *Puha* enveloped the earth in a great network, much like a spider's web and held the earth together. It was and remains the original power among *Nuwuvi* people. *Puha* had intelligence, will, and the ability to give itself to or withdraw itself from people, places, plants, and animals. *Puha* sat in places near and far within the storied landscapes of Southern Paiute people, including high mountains where clouds hovered bringing life-giving moisture that fed the earth with water. *Puha* existed in springs, ponds, lakes, and rivers like the Colorado, Virgin, and Armargosa Rivers. At Chemehuevi Valley, power flowed in and with the Colorado River, which streamed red in color just east of the village. *Puha* concentrated at *Hawaiyo*, West Well, located a few miles west of Chemehuevi Valley where the ancient and Little People created petroglyphs and pictographs. Most important, *puha* attached itself to certain men and women, empowering them to be healers, holy people, and psychics who used their gift of spiritual power to benefit the people.

Ceremonies allowed the *Nuwuvi* people to tangibly express elements of their spiritual beliefs. Some common ones include the *Yagapi* or Cry Ceremonies, where the songs of the community send deceased loved ones to their next existence in the Milky Way. The *Yagapi* was and remains a ceremony of beautiful sadness as the family and mourners of the deceased gather to sing ceremonial Salt Songs. The Salt

Song ceremony guides the spirit of the dead to steps leading to *Nuva Kiav,* the hole in the sky and the entryway into the heavens. Just a part of the *Nuwuvi* cosmology, the Salt Songs and other spiritual stories were told over and over again to tribal children, who gathered at night to listen and learn "with both ears" so they might know the origin of all things *Nuwuvi*. As with all civilizations, at the center of concern was the question of life's meaning: why are we here, what is life for, why must we suffer and die. And understanding the significance of life and death formed a core of *Nuwuvi* beliefs. Following the creation of humans, people on earth experienced a time for living and then death. Initially the souls of the dead had nowhere to go and their ghosts remained on earth in spirit form, which posed potential danger for the living. Some souls were malevolent and could do harm, bringing imbalance, sickness, and death to human societies.

Once again, Coyote figures into the *Nuwuvi* worldview. Traveling around Snow Mountain some time after the creation of human beings, Coyote noticed many ghosts inhabiting space between earth and the afterlife. Coyote had seen these souls of the dead before, though he hadn't given them much thought. But as more and more people died, the space inhabited by ghosts was getting increasingly congested. In a moment of inspiration Coyote realized that souls had nowhere to go – Ocean Woman and her agents had not planned on a place for the souls of the dead. Coyote consulted his brother, Wolf, and together they designed a destination plan for the souls of the dead: they would live in a sky world within the Milky Way, removed from close proximity to the earth where they were interfering with human life. The entryway into the heavens was situated at the site of ascendancy on the northern face of Snow Mountain, forming a hole in the sky from which souls would travel into the Milky Way. To make things easier for *Nuwuvi* souls, Coyote used his saliva to make steps leading to *Nuva Kiav,* the Hole in the Sky. To aid the souls of the dead in finding their way to *Nuva Kiav,* Coyote and Wolf composed a series of songs as a sort of guidepost. These songs described the path for souls traveling to the Hole in the Sky, as well as a trail followed by grieving humans to help them go on with life on earth.

In his childhood and youth, Willie Boy would have learned of the origin of the Salt Songs through the story of Wolf and Coyote, who placed songs in a sacred cave called *Ting-i-ai* located east of the Colorado River upstream on the Bill Williams River in Western Arizona. These stories described two sisters (*Yárik* or Wild Goose and *Avínankawats* or Small Duck-Like) traveling westward down the Bill Williams River. In need of rest, the sisters selected a cave to sleep, unknowingly choosing *Ting-i-ai,* the holy cave where Wolf and Coyote had placed the sacred songs to guide the souls of the dead into the heavens. You might anticipate the women would be punished for violating a sacred space, but the night spent in *Ting-i-ai* brought about a transformative change for the two sisters. In the course of their resting, each woman received specific spiritual knowledge through *Asihuvwiyavi* or Salt Songs, as well as a spiritual charge to use the songs to establish the Salt Song Trail. While following the trail of 1000 miles, singing the holy songs as they moved along, the Sisters passed deposits of salt, composed of the salty tears shed by those mourning the loss of loved ones.

At every *Yagapi* Ceremony, or wake Willie Boy and other Chemehuevi attended, he heard Salt Songs sung from dusk till dawn. These songs were burned into the people's minds through frequent repetition, creating a record as accurate as any written down with ink and paper. The Spirit Speaker would say, "when the Creator gave us these songs, He told us He would give us beautiful songs, but in order for you to know these songs, I must break your heart." Salt Songs led souls of the dead on a long musical journey from *Ting-i-ai* down the Bill Williams River to its junction with the Colorado River, east into the Hualapai Country, and north across the Colorado River. The songs took the Sisters into Southern Paiute villages and west to Las Vegas before traveling a short distance to the north side of Snow Mountain where the Sisters parted, one beginning her journey up the stairway to *Nuva Kiav* and the other remaining on earth. Those attending the wakes sang Salt Songs, especially at midnight when everyone sang the Cry Song before taking a break. The *Yagapi* Ceremonies sent the souls of their loved ones into the next world. Only one sister, the one representing life on earth, continued her journey south of the Spring Mountains on the Salt Song Trail. The songs traveled with the remaining sister south to Ash Meadows, Red Ant Hill, and the Oasis of Mara at the present-day site of the city of Twentynine Palms, California. The Oasis of Mara, an Indian village composed of Serrano and Chemehuevi Indians, was well-known to Willie Boy, whose grandmothers, aunts, and cousins lived at the Indian village at the Oasis of Mara, on the property today of the 29 Palms Inn.

    The Salt Song Trail continued south of Twenty-Nine Palms toward Palm Springs, east to the Colorado River and turned north past the Giant Intaglios north of Blythe, California. Farther north at the Riverside Mountains, the lone sister swam to the Arizona side of the river. On the east side of the Colorado River, she entered the Parker Valley near present-day Poston, Arizona, where other Chemehuevi people lived. The young woman traveled north toward the Whipple and Buckskin Mountains before following the Bill Williams River east to *Ting-i-ai* where the Salt Song Trail began and ended. Salt Song Singers shared their last songs during the grey dawn just before the sun rose as villagers prepared to bury their loved one. The ceremony concluded with a morning feast shared among the grieving loved ones. During the all-night Salt Song Ceremony, everyone in attendance relived the first Salt Song journey, which brought healing and renewal to the people. The Salt Songs brought to life once again the deep belief system of the ancient ones, the ancestors who first followed the Salt Song Trail through mountains, deserts, and valleys to arrive at *Nuva Kiav*.

In the traditional lifeway of the *Nuwuvi,* practical skills were as important as ceremonial knowledge. Bows and arrows were constructed by hand and used to hunt small animals with arrows whittled into a point and tempered hard in a fire. Male elders also guided boys in the use of blunt-tipped arrows to spar with each other as they learned protection skills. Elder hunters, accompanied by young apprentice hunters, tracked and killed deer, bighorn sheep, rabbits, fowl, and other animals the people ate. Men controlled the hunting domain and became expert with a bow and, later, a rifle, from a young age.

As a child, Willie Boy accompanied his mother, Mary Snyder, into the desert and nearby mountains to gather agave, yucca, chia, mesquite, cactus, and a host of other plant foods. Women, girls, and small children did most of the gathering, collecting many varieties of plant food they processed, stored, and cooked throughout the seasons. Willie Boy and other boys eventually took their place with the men, traveling the ancient trails deep into the desert and mountains. Older men sang "song maps," which they used to travel trails leading to water and promising hunting or gathering grounds and that mapped the desert and mountainous landscape. Hunters traveled the mountains and deserts with hollow tubes made of cane, which they used like straws to take water from tiny seeps found in rocks. They taught the young men to track, kill, and dress animals in many ways, while also giving thanks at shrines along the desert floor and mountain trails. Stopping at rock piles to add a stone, stick, tobacco, or sage, the men offered a prayer for the safety and wellbeing of the travelers. When men made hunting camps at springs, they told stories about former hunts, wars, notable people, sacred places, and the way *puha* sat in powerful places. At night, they reported that they heard faint singing, melodies floating in the wind sung by spirits. Other times they heard pecking on the rocks from Little People carving into rocks and making rock drawings known today as petroglyphs.

    As a youngster, tribal elders sensed that Willie Boy had a special ability as a runner, a valuable person within the Indian communities. To communicate with other Indians, tribal leaders depended on runners to travel swiftly on foot to other villages with news and knowledge, intelligence necessary to protect the people from invasions or to organize councils. As a child, Willie Boy distinguished himself as an athlete with perfect eyesight and agile body. He had great stamina and an innate ability to track animals and men. He could outrun and kill animals better than most others. Willie Boy won footraces in contests with other boys and, later, men. As a result of his unusual running ability, older runners recruited him into the Chemehuevi society of runners to serve his community as a magical runner. He grew up among runners and learned a secret way of running, including the ability to run in the "old way." Chemehuevi believed these special runners could fly.

Southern Paiute people believed that master runners like Willie Boy held a special power or *puha* that allowed them to fly from place to place, thereby running in the old way. This specialized form of running was a well-kept secret, even among the *Nuwuvi*, known only to runners and never shared with others. Older Chemehuevi runners shared their secrets when Willie Boy joined their ranks. Willie Boy became an extraordinary runner possessing special powers. Chemehuevi elder Mary Lou Brown once explained that Willie "ran in the old way, for he was like the wind." To this day, American Indian people from different Native nations describe Willie Boy as one of the gifted Chemehuevi runners who understood the terrain and had a unique way of running: he could leave the earth and arrive at his appointed destination in an accelerated amount of time.

As white settlement encroached on Indian lands, newcomers arrived from other parts of the United States and from Mexico, Australia, China, and many other foreign countries. During the last two decades of the nineteenth century and first decade of the twentieth century, Willie Boy and other *Nuwuvi* watched as settlers, miners, merchants, ranchers, and farmers moved west looking for new opportunities on Indian lands. Settler communities brought new religions, towns, foreign governments, agents, land thefts, reservations, and alcohol. Willie Boy lived at a complicated time for Native American communities. Newcomers eager to exploit Native American lands and resources disrupted Indian traditions and lifeways, both by infringing on Native life and by offering non-Native opportunities for *Nuwuvi* people. Each of these alternatives proved disruptive. Times were changing in the late nineteenth and early twentieth centuries, and Willie Boy witnessed radical and rapid change all around him.

    Willie Boy grew up in the old way, but he could see the impact settlers had on the lives of all Native Americans. The mere presence of settlers and their ever-growing numbers threatened the traditional lives of Indian people. American soldiers had fought a series of wars against American Indians in the western United States, and American policy makers had forced tribal people to live on reservations, concentrating Native Americans on confined areas and not permitting them to hunt, gather, and fish in their usual and accustomed areas. Day and boarding schools run by white people separated Indian children from their parents to reprogram them from their "savage ways" to "civilized" human beings. White educators attempted to drum indigenous languages, cultures, and religions out of small children. Willie Boy never attended these schools, but he lived and worked among settlers and learned the English language by interacting with English speakers. That life – one in which a Native person lived near and worked with settlers – was an alternative to living on one of the Indian reservations created by the government. Early on the United States limited the Native estate dividing Indian lands into allotments and selling off large portions of Indian land to settlers. These newcomers harmed natural materials used to make baskets, bows, arrows, lodges, and a host of other material items *Nuwuvi* people had known since the time of Ocean Woman. Witnessing the destruction of Indian cultures and ways of life, it's no surprise that some Indian people searched for power to counter the influences of settlers.

In the late nineteenth century, a messenger emerged on the scene, a holy man from among Northern Paiute people offering hope and innovative thinking. The new religious movement was a direct retort to the growing number of settlers and the invasion of Indian Country by land hungry newcomers. Besides the soldiers, miners, merchants, ranchers, and agents, American Indians faced an onslaught of zealous missionaries, ministers, and do-gooders who denigrated Native American cultures, languages, and spiritual beliefs. They came to Indian country to reshape Indians into "civilized" people. Conversion to Christianity was a primary goal, even though Christianity emerged in a foreign country, a world away from Native America. Indian people learned of Christian tenets of peace, forgiveness, and a new kingdom – many adopted this religion while maintaining their traditional beliefs as well. But as an alternative religion, one emerging from Native people and offering a message of hope and forward-thinking. In 1890, Willie Boy learned of an indigenous faith that had developed years before among indigenous of western Nevada and eastern California. On January 1, 1889, a Paiute man named Wovoka (Cutter) experienced heavenly revelations by dying and traveling to the spirit world, where the Creator instructed Wovoka in a new faith and instructed him to perform dances, songs, and rituals. At first, Wovoka shared his message with the *Numu* or Northern Paiute people as well as Shoshone people. Very quickly, this new religious practice radiated out in all directions, reaching the *Nuwuvi* and Yuman people. Willie Boy joined in the new Indian religion.

    Native Americans gave the new spiritual movement many names, but it is best known as the Ghost Dance. Drawing on the information gained in his afterlife experience, Wovoka crafted the message provided by the Father into a religious ceremony involving dancing, singing, and religious ritual. Wovoka, the Ghost Dance Prophet, described his near-death experience: his spirit had traveled to the Father, who instructed Wovoka to return to the people and tell them to sing and dance "at intervals for five consecutive days" to hasten an Indian apocalypse. The earth would transform into an Indian paradise, where Native people would be situated within their own homelands.

The Ghost Dance Prophet preached world renewal, envisioning a pure environment filled with game and productive plants, clean and plentiful water. The Creator, Ghost Dancers believed, would bring about a new millennium for Native Americans free of white people. And until the great apocalypse, Indians must sing, dance, and conduct ceremony while living in peace and love with others, including white people. And astonishingly, in an era of discrimination and diminishing opportunities to live in traditional ways, Indian people were to forsake hatred, quarreling, stealing, and "put away the old practices that favored war."

Chemehuevi called the new religion *Nikapi* or Circle Dance, but Willie Boy knew that white people identified the faith as the Ghost Dance. Non-Indians watched Indian followers of *Nikapi* sing and dance several days and nights in a row, making participants look ghostly during the long hours spent dancing in a circle. As individual dancers executed the dance steps, the Spirit moved with them; in fact, the Spirit remained with faithful followers for weeks or months following the ceremony. The Ghost Dance belief in the power of the Spirit matched that of the Southern Paiute belief in *puha,* the network of intelligent and willful spiritual power flowing into the lives of participants of holy gatherings.

In 1890, Ghost Dancers among the Northern Paiute sent a sacred pipe to various bands of Southern Paiute. From one group of Southern Paiute to another, the pipe circulated and eventually reached Chemehuevi villages located on both sides of the Colorado River near present-day Havasu Landing. Each village smoked the sacred pipe, praying for good things to come to *Nuwuvi* communities. According to a Chemehuevi elder living at the time, the sacred pipe circulated among all *Nuwuvi* people, including those living in Chemehuevi Valley on the California side of the river. A leader named *Kuyuuti* carried the pipe from Chemehuevi Valley to *Nuwuvi* living in Needles. *Kuyuuti* brought word that while many people believed a Great Fire would destroy the world, participants in the *Nikapi* or Chemehuevi Ghost Dance would be saved, dancing and singing above the fire in preparation of a new age. *Kuyuuti* also told the people to listen to the heavens, for they would surely hear the voice of the Grandfather or Father, the One Above. Some elders reported hearing a voice coming from the sky, a message from the Creator.

In Willie Boy's youth, the Ghost Dance came among *Nuwuvi* people, offering new ideas and beliefs. As Willie Boy participated in the Ghost Dance religion, he joined in the *Nikapi* Ceremony in Chemehuevi Valley and likely elsewhere along the river and in the villages of the Mojave Desert. This was a life-altering experience for the young man, opening his world to new people, new ideas, and new ways of thinking about life on earth. And it went beyond the Ghost Dance practice – Willie Boy came of age in the new century, when non-Indians influenced many aspects of Chemehuevi life, for better and for worse. When traditional Indian economies began to collapse, indigenous men and women ventured out from reservations and their communities to seek employment in new settlements. Willie Boy was no different, relocating to white settlements where work could be found. It was a deviation from the traditional ways of the Southern Paiute, where focus on villages, communities, and family was the paramount concern. When Willie Boy found work as a cowboy in Victorville, California, exposure to the ways of white people inevitably influenced his view of life during a changing time. Perhaps most notably was a shifting mindset away from traditional culture and an embrace of a more individual-centered value system.

Like heroic characters in the stories of Chemehuevi, Willie Boy left his home in Chemehuevi Valley to seek adventure. His sister, Georgia, had set an example by moving to the frontier town of Victorville in the western part of San Bernardino County. Around 1900, Willie Boy journeyed across the Mojave Desert on foot, likely singing his map songs to guide him along ancient trails leading deep into the desert. Decades of geographical knowledge among the *Nuwuvi* proved advantageous to finding springs and seeps as he made his way to the Mojave River. A hollowed piece of cane helped procure water from those secluded water sources. Food was also to be found in the desert, including the tiny chia seeds for quick energy and to expand in their stomachs, creating a sense of fullness. Chia seeds are composed of water, protein, and fat. Chemehuevi runners easily carried the seeds in a leather pouch that they tied around their waist so they could wet their fingers, place them in the bag, and bring forth many small chia seeds to feed their bodies and boost their energy. On his way to Victorville, Willie Boy gathered other plant foods and hunted small animals. He knew the desert and he knew how to survive.

Willie Boy was one with the desert, running like the wind and guided by the stars and the trail before him. A *Nuwuvi* runner like Willie Boy could travel many miles by day and by night. Arriving safely in Victorville, Willie Boy joined his sister in time to take part in the 1900 United States Census. That census recorded that Willie Boy had taken custody of two orphaned Indian boys from another tribe, including "Indian Bill" eight years old, and "Indian Albert" six years old. But little else is known about Willie Boy's days in Victorville, except for his arrest for disorderly conduct. A fist fight broke out between Indian and non-Indian baseball players, and lawmen arrested Willie Boy for disturbing the peace. He served between 20 and 40 days in jail, time which undoubtedly soured his taste for Victorville. With his two orphans in tow, Willie Boy moved east over 85 miles to the Chemehuevi and Serrano village of Twenty-Nine Palms, known to Indians as the Oasis of Mara.

For over forty years, Chemehuevi and Serrano Indians had lived in peace with each other. The Oasis of Mara (also known as "Little Spring, Much Grass" to its Native inhabitants) was the origin site and longtime center for Serrano Indians. According to contemporary Serrano leader Ernest Siva, "the *Maarrenga'yam* were brought to *Maarra'* by *Cheenep* (our Lord) from the other world, *Maarra'*. We floated here through space. Our story was told in the Bird Songs." Serrano people established their village on the north side of the tree line at the present-day site of the 29 Palms Inn. As settlers moved into the region, traditionally held Indian land was sold off to the highest bidders, and the area around the Oasis of Mara was no exception. In the twentieth century, the Grunt family purchased and consistently protected the village site where the Indians built their homes and enjoyed the fruits of a large garden. Preventing construction on the site has protected the integrity of this sacred place on the Salt Song Trail.

    At the Oasis of Mara, Chemehuevi and Serrano formed bonds of friendship and alliance. By the first decade of the twentieth century, they had settled into a positive and nurturing relationship in the isolated village. In fact, it became something of a draw for aging Chemehuevi elders from small communities in the Mojave Desert. In the late nineteenth and early twentieth century, villages among the desert Chemehuevi, known as the *Tiraniwiwi,* vacated their former homelands. Young people, like Georgia and Willie Boy moved into towns or ranches to work and experience a new life among the *Haiko* (settlers). Once young people moved away from desert villages, elders moved into Twenty-Nine Palms to live out their final years. These tribal elders were cared for at the Oasis of Mara by younger members of the Serrano and Chemehuevi community.

    Willie Boy and his two boys traveled across the high desert from Victorville to the Oasis of Mara. Willie Boy knew the trails and important landmarks, especially the location of water sources. The trail they followed took them along the northern edge of the San Bernardino Mountains, populated with oak, piñon, and pine trees. For centuries, Chemehuevi, Cahuilla, and Serrano people gathered acorns and piñons in the mountains, and hunted deer, bighorn sheep, squirrels, rabbits, and other mammals in the mountains. In keeping with Native tradition, the *Yahaviatum* Band of Serrano Indians owned the mountains through their hereditary songs. When Chemehuevi or Cahuilla Indians wanted to hunt and gather in these lands, they asked the *keeka* or chief of the *Yahaviatum* Band for permission to hunt or gather. During

Willie Boy's lifetime, *Keeka Pakuuma* or Santos Manuel led this band of Serrano. He was a generous and friendly man as well as a powerful shaman and civil leader.

    Willie Boy's trek with the orphans east across the Mojave Desert was a dress rehearsal for his escape from the posse a few years in the future. Keeping a memory of the places they encountered, especially sources of water, would prove useful as the posse chased him into the far reaches of the Mojave Desert. The old Indian trail followed by Willie Boy and the two orphan boys paralleled present-day state route 247. Moving southeast past present-day sites of Apple Valley and Lucerne Valley, the travelers passed Rabbit Springs where on February 16, 1867, militia soldiers from San Bernardino attacked and killed peaceful Chemehuevi men, women, and children. They encountered the massive Giant Rock and Chimney Rock, unforgettable sites standing not far from the Blackhawk Landslides. And near present-day Landers, California, Willie Boy and the two orphans passed Ruby Mountain, a site destined to figure prominently in the runner's life, and in the legends about Willie Boy passed down from 1909 to the present.

    From Landers, the well-worn Indian trail continued east to the present site of Joshua Tree and Highway 62. Not far to the east was the Oasis of Mara, where a line of Washington palm trees lined the landscape and large pockets of water were trapped in an underground reservoir. At the close of the Ice Age, Native Americans lived at the Oasis of Mara because of the abundance of water, game, and plant life. Although Serrano people had lived at Twenty-Nine Palms since time immemorial, Willie Boy's people had only recently settled the area in the 1860s. His grandmother and grandfather, the Ticup family, lived there now and would welcome their grandson and the orphans he brought to the oasis.

Willie Boy originally lodged with his grandmother, Mrs. Ticup, and his aunts in a *samarókwai,* a permanent home made of logs, sticks, adobe, and palm fronds. Unlike the river Chemehuevi who used a great deal of arrowweed, the desert people commonly used palm fronds in their construction of houses, shaded ramadas, and lean-to structures attached to many homes. On top of some of the houses or on stilts, women made large granary baskets filled with plant foods stored high above the ground to prevent rats, mice, squirrels, and other animals from eating their stores of food. At times, Willie Boy's mother, Mary Snyder, also lived periodically at the Oasis of Mara, though she was not a permanent resident.

The oasis was well-named. In the shade of the palm trees, small ponds of water stood along the line of palm trees. Birds and small mammals took advantage of the desert water source, living in the grove of palm trees. And a small distance from the oasis, homes sat on a sandy plain and the shallow downward slope from the palm trees. The young orphans would have eagerly played along the tree line with other children of the Chemehuevi and Serrano residents. An elderly man spent his days hunting small animals for food, which he shot with his bow and gave to the families living at the oasis. It was in many ways an idyllic retreat from the confusion and pressures of white towns and enterprises.

At the oasis, Willie Boy crossed paths with his cousin Carlota, the sixteen-year-old daughter of William and Maria Mike. William Mike was no one to under-estimate: he was the *Thau Winthum* or chief of Chemehuevi at Twenty-Nine Palms and a shaman, a man to whom spirits bestowed power to lead ceremonies and heal people. More to the point,

William Mike was an intimidating figure. He governed the Chemehuevi of the Twenty-Nine Palms Band with a "big stick," keeping the villagers in line to follow traditional "laws" or norms of the people. Far from tolerating missteps from his sons and daughters, William Mike expected his children to set an example for everyone in the village.

By Chemehuevi standards of 1900, Carlota was a woman of marrying age. She had experienced her puberty ceremony and the elder women had taught her the responsibilities of womanhood. Carlota has been described as a beauty, possessing long black hair, a slightly round face with big dark eyes and a petite nose, all complemented with a charming personality. Carlota was full of life, a young woman with lots of energy and a commitment to please her elders and follow the rules of her strict father. Which was a good thing, as her father expected much of his daughters, especially that they follow *Nuwuvi* laws, including rules pertaining to marriage.

In the early 20th century, *Nuwuvi* parents still played matchmaker in the selection of their children's spouses. Who better to ensure a proper partnership based on traditional values rather than impulsive attraction? And traditional values were often stringent: in order to marry, the couple had to be unrelated by five or six generations. Chief William Mike adhered to this law, insisting on approving the suitors of all his children to keep his family line pure. Willie Boy would be an unsuitable choice for Carlota on several counts. Twelve years her senior, a recent arrival at the oasis from white settlements, and a relative. For Carlota, these were minor obstacles in her pursuit of Willie Boy.

So why was Carlota attracted to the young man who her parents deemed an unacceptable match? Perhaps it was Willie Boy's handsome features, maturity, athleticism, and experience. The attractions were many: Carlota recognized in Willie Boy a superior athlete, one of the elite runners of *Nuwuvi* people in the many bands of Southern Paiute living in Nevada, Utah, Arizona, and California. He was physically attractive in a mysterious, appealing sort of way. Most apparent was his thin frame, medium height, and obvious agility with a muscular body and dark cropped hair adding to his allure. His dark, penetrating eyes spoke to Willie Boy's leadership qualities. A reserved but confident young man, he dressed well and maintained a tasteful appearance. Reports from those who knew him paint a picture of a man who rarely raised his voice, didn't boast or brag, and worked hard. He was a crack shot with a gun and a successful hunter. There was much about Willie Boy to admire, and it's hard to imagine Carlota was the only young girl to show an interest in the young man.

When Willie Boy moved to the Chemehuevi village at Twenty-Nine Palms, he appeared to have left his life of individualism to reenter the cooperative, communal life of *Nuwuvi* people. At the oasis, Willie Boy contributed to the community by hunting, tending the garden, hauling water, and splitting firewood. The village at Twenty-Nine Palms was not large, and Willie knew everyone living at the oasis, including the Chemehuevi leader, William Mike and Jim Pine who oversaw the Serrano people. William was a big man, gentle, humorous, and kind on the one hand while also projecting an intimidating sternness. In his youth, William Mike had fought Mojave Indians, rose to a leadership position, and was known to be dangerous if provoked. As an adult, he fathered a large family, including Carlota who developed a romantic interest in Willie Boy. The attraction between the two young people set in motion a series of tragic, violent events. The ultimate carnage would touch the lives of every member of both Willie Boy's and Carlota's families.

Fig. 14—Remains of Grand Mesa in Chemehuevis Valley.

In 1858, Lieutenant Joseph Christmas Ives and a few soldiers explored the Colorado River in the steamboat *Explorer*. Artist Heinrich Bauduin Möllhausen made this sketch of Chemehuevi Valley, the site of the largest Chemehuevi Indian village. William and Maria Mike as well as Willie Boy were born in Chemehuevi Valley in the shadow of the Chemehuevi Mountains. J.C. Ives, "Report on the Colorado River of the West," *Report of the Secretary of War, 1861*, sketch by Heinrich Bauduin Möllhausen.

When Willie Boy and other Chemehuevi traveled from Chemehuevi Valley to the Oasis of Mara, along the way they traveled near or through the Old Woman Mountains located forty miles west of the Colorado River. Author's Photograph.

In 1853 and 1854, Lieutenant Joseph Christmas Ives conducted a survey of the 35th Parallel Route. He crossed the Colorado River near the present site of Fort Mojave where he met Mojave and Chemehuevi warriors. Artist Heinrich Bauduin Möllhausen sketched this illustration of a Chemehuevi warrior with a short hunting bow. A. W. Whipple, "Reports of Explorations and Surveys, to Ascertain the Most Practicable and Economical Route for a Railroad from the Mississippi River to the Pacific Ocean," *Senate Executive Document 78*, 33rd Congress, 2nd Session, 1856.

A collection of Chemehuevi baskets made by masterful women of the Chemehuevi Tribe appears here. Many women at Twenty-Nine Palms and Chemehuevi Valley were artists trained by elder women to make beautiful and utilitarian baskets. Courtesy Gerald Smith Collection, Archives, A. K. Smiley Library, Redlands, California.

Willie Boy's mother, *So Iris* or Mary Snyder, was a master basket maker. She was a woman of power and made the famous rattlesnake basket without danger to herself. Tribal member Wilene Holt Fisher took this photograph of a basket from the Colorado River Indian Tribes Museum Collections. Courtesy of Wilene Holt Fisher.

In 1897, basket makers living in the village of Twenty-Nine Palms posed for this photograph, depicting their basket making abilities. They were superior artists who wove baskets for use by their families and to sell to tourist through Indian traders. Courtesy of Paul Smith.

This large, exquisite basket is a superior example of the artistry of Chemehuevi women. This is a granary basket, used to hold mesquite beans for a family. Courtesy Gerald Smith Collection, Archives, A. K. Smiley Library, Redlands, California.

Chemehuevi people lived in a variety of housing types, including A-framed homes like the one in this picture made of poles and thatched with arrowweed. Courtesy Gerald Smith Collection, Archives, A. K. Smiley Library.

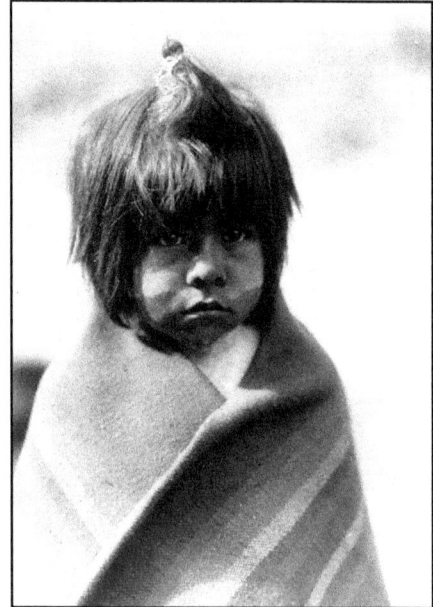

This photograph by famed photographer Edward Curtis is titled, "Chemehuevi Boy With Painted Face." Notice the manufactured blanket he wears and the way his mother tied up his hair. He is prepared to participate in a dance, sing, or ceremony. Courtesy Gerald Smith Collection, Archives, A. K. Smiley Library.

The Serrano and Chemehuevi of Twenty-Nine Palms located their village on the north side of the tree line of Washingtonian Palm trees that were native to the Oasis of Mara. Today the 29 Palms Inn is located on the land once the home of desert Serrano and Chemehuevi. Author's Photograph.

Randolph Madison, a newspaper reporter, took this photograph of William and Maria Mike. The photograph shows their mud and daub home as well as the ceremonial lodge to the right where Chemehuevi held *Yagapi* Ceremonies. Maria is holding their youngest child, Dorothy. Courtesy Harry Lawton Collection, Rivera Library, University of California, Riverside.

In 1909, Maria Mike and her family worked on the Gilman Ranch in Banning, California, at the time Willie Boy killed William Mike. Here Maria is working among the fruit trees with three of her children. Maria is holding baby Dorothy. Courtesy Harry Lawton Collection, Rivera Library, University of California, Riverside.

Maria Mike is facing the camera of Randolph Madison of the *Los Angeles Record*, a newspaper reporter assigned to write on the Willie Boy affair. Harry Lawton Collection, Rivera Library, University of California, Riverside.

Albert and Sam Mike, two sons of William Mike, worked drying fruit in the Banning Pass, most likely on the Gilman Ranch. In 1916, San Bernardino City Police murdered the two boys for drinking. In 1909, reporter Randolph Madison took this photograph of these two Mike boys. Courtesy Harry Lawton Collection, Rivera Library, University of California, Riverside.

Billy Mike was a son of Jim Mike and nephew of William Mike. He married Nellie Holms Mike. After Billy's death from a gunshot wound, Nellie married John Morongo. Billy is seen in this photograph working in the orchards at the Gilman Ranch. He was at the ranch when Willie Boy killed William Mike. Courtesy Harry Lawton Collection, Rivera Library, University of California, Riverside.

Nellie Mike married Billy Mike when the two lived at the Indian village at the Oasis of Mara. Nellie was at the village after the gun battle between the posse and Willie Boy. When Willie Boy returned to the village at Twenty-Nine Palms, Nellie watched his interactions with his grandmother and later shared an oral history about Willie Boy's last known visit to the oasis community. Courtesy Harry Lawton Collection, Rivera Library, University of California, Riverside.

Jim Pine led the Serrano community at the Oasis of Mara as a partner to William Mike. He is seen here with his wife, Matilda, at their home at the village of Twenty-Nine Palms. The Serrano Big House or Ceremonial Lodge existed adjacent to Jim's home. According to Dorothy Ramon, in 1910, Chemehuevi, Serrano, and Cahuilla helped Jim move the Big House to Mission Creek. Courtesy Harry Lawton Collection, Rivera Library, University of California, Riverside.

Chapter 2
William, Willie, and Carlota

In 1844 or 1855, William Mike was born in the Chemehuevi Valley on the western bank along the Colorado River in an indigenous space that became the eastern border of California. At that time, more Chemehuevi lived in this *Nuwuvi* village than any other. The people had selected a productive desert setting for their home with rich silt from the river and ample water to nurture their crops. Plants and animals lived in profusion on and near the Colorado River of the West. The Indian village in Chemehuevi Valley faced east toward the rising sun, the Mohave Mountains in Arizona, and the Colorado River. Across the river on the eastern bank as far as the eye could see to the north and south stood several grand mountain ranges of rocks and sand. In fact, several rocky monuments cradled the village in Chemehuevi Valley, providing beauty every day as the sun passed over the place from east to west. The angle of light animated the desert, splashing the landscape with light bringing ever-changing colors onto the rugged mountain ranges, valleys, and shadows in between. Within this grand environment, Chemehuevi found foods from plants and animals. At one time, bighorn sheep, deer, desert tortoises, rabbits, and pronghorn populated the region. Over the years, Chemehuevi memorialized these animals through songs and stories, including Deer and Bighorn Sheep Songs. These two animals played a major role in oral narratives and songs, because people revered the animals they ate, giving thanks to the Creator for nature's gifts.

William Mike was born into the Timtimmon family, which was also called the Timpemoningtit or

Timpingmoneytite family. English speaking people called the family by the name, Mike, which became the preferred surname of family members. William Mike's youth was rooted in the traditional manner and ancient religion of his people. Tribal elders taught him songs and stories through the oral tradition. He hunted animals, large and small, and he learned to fight. Some elders say that the great hunters could talk to game animals and lure them to the hunter through their thoughts, songs, and prayers. But during this same period, William Mike witnessed an increasingly tumultuous time. American settlers first migrated into the American West after the War between the United States and Mexico, with numbers increasing yearly. Settlers added a new element to a tenuous relationship between Chemehuevi and Mojave Indians.

Mojave people lived nearby Chemehuevi in villages to the north, south, and east of Chemehuevi Valley. The Mojave living in the desert to the west of Chemehuevi Valley posed a potential threat to *Nuwuvi* people based on sheer numbers. Newcomers had entered the region during William's youth, exploring the desert in all directions. As the Army Corps of Engineers surveyed roads going west, settlers followed. In 1858, when William was about 14, one group of American soldiers under the command of Lieutenant Joseph Christmas Ives, brought the first steamboat, *Explorer,* up the Colorado River. As the Ives expedition traveled through Chemehuevi country on their little steamboat, Indian people watched in delight. Ives took the *Explorer* as far north on the river as El Dorado Canyon where in the 1930s engineers situated Hoover Dam. Lieutenant Ives produced a detailed report of the Colorado River region, offering a good deal of information on the life, culture, and physical appearance of Chemehuevi men and women.

The arrival of the United States Army on the Colorado River led to a body of rich ethnographical information for future generations of settlers. However, for William Mike, his family, and Indian people in general, the arrival of soldiers signaled the building of forts on the river and the continual presence of a new and potentially dangerous people. Chemehuevi carefully navigated their relationship with the Army at Fort Yuma and Fort Mojave, but the Mojave Indians challenged the right of American settlers to cross the Colorado River and travel through Mojave territory. A group of highly skilled Mojave warriors attacked an American wagon train trying to cross the river, successfully driving them east. The Indian victory triggered a federal response, with the United States Army challenging Mojave warriors with guns, horses, and the force of army troops. Many Mojave died as federal forces defeated tribal warriors. In the wake of the battle, the army-built Fort Mojave on the banks of the Colorado River near present-day Needles, California. Fort Mojave provided a base for soldiers and protection for settlers on their way to California.

William Mike and his fellow *Nuwuvi* remained out of the fray with the United States Army, but the presence of American soldiers destabilized the balance of power between Chemehuevi and Mojave, ultimately leading to several years of war between the tribes. Mojave leaders blamed the Chemehuevi. *Nuwuvi* people blamed the Mojave. In a series of skirmishes and battles during the 1860s, the two peoples fought and killed each other in pitched battles. On a national level, Mojave Chief Irataba met with American officials in Los Angeles and later traveled to Washington, D.C., to visit President Abraham Lincoln, who gifted Irataba a cane as a sign of respect. Lincoln promised Irataba he would recognize a reservation for Mojave people and these plans were set in motion before he died at Ford's Theater from an assassin's bullet. Nevertheless, on March 3, 1866, the United States recognized the Colorado River Indian Reservation, which included a large landscape of present-day Parker Valley in Arizona as well as a strip of land in California. William Mike was a young man of about twenty during these developments. He had fought the Mojave as a warrior, demonstrating his leadership ability. A conservative young man and ardent supporter of Chemehuevi culture, language, and autonomy, he believed in the ancient spiritual beliefs of *Nuwuvi* people, and the spiritual world gifted him the ability to heal others. William Mike cherished Chemehuevi sovereignty and did not want to live on a reservation under the thumb of the United States or Mojave leaders.

When Irataba brought his people south into the Parker Valley, some Mojave remained in the north. The people who followed Irataba adopted the spelling, Mohave to distinguish themselves from their relatives at Fort Mojave. Initially, the government intended the Colorado Indian Reservation to be the home of Mohave people, but in the nineteenth century, government agents placed Chemehuevi, Yavapai, and Hualapai Indians on the same reservation. In the twentieth century, the government saw fit to consign Hopi and Navajo people to the Colorado River Indian Reservation as well, where the confederated tribes remain today. That outcome did not sit well with some *Nuwuvi,* and when federal agents crossed the Colorado River to urge the people living at Chemehuevi Valley to move onto the Colorado River Indian Reservation, the more conservative *Nuwuvi* refused and found other places to live. Some Chemehuevi refused to move onto the newly established Colorado River Indian Reservation where Mohave people would constitute the majority. In the late 1860s, some Chemehuevi remained at war with the Mohave and did not trust they would be safe on the reservation.

As a result, conservative and independent *Nuwuvi*, including the family and followers of Jim and William Mike, moved west into the heart of the Mojave Desert. In the 1860s and 1870s, Chemehuevi experienced a major diaspora as their population scattered to avoid consignment on the Colorado River Indian Reservation. Some Chemehuevi bands moved into the Mojave Desert to live near mountain ranges where they could hunt and near water sources where they farmed small plots. Others migrated to the valley along the Mojave River. *Carriota*, for example, led his family and others on a journey west using ancient trails identified in the song maps, ultimately arriving at the Oasis of Mara, the home of Serrano people. Some Chemehuevi traveled as far as the Pacific Ocean, while others hunted and gathered in the San Bernardino Mountains. To their advantage, they knew the topography and used that knowledge to their benefit.

During the 1860s, the Mike family emerged as major leaders of one group of Chemehuevi, especially *Carriota* or Jim Mike, William's older brother. William had earned a reputation as a smart and effective young warrior during the Mojave-Chemehuevi Wars. As mentioned before, William Mike had distinguished himself as a leader of young warriors and became a man of spiritual healing power. The senior member of the Mike family, however, was the older brother Jim, who also served as leader of one band of Chemehuevi people. Jim married Neitta (also known as María or Mary but not to be confused with another woman named Maria who married William Mike). According to the Mike family, both brothers preferred to be known as the Mike family. The extended Mike family also included Maria's widowed mother, Surda, who was among the great Chemehuevi basket makers. Surda lived with William and Maria, helping with their children as the family grew. During the 1860s in the aftermath of the Chemehuevi-Mojave War and creation of the Colorado River Indian Reservations in the valley near Parker, Arizona, Jim and William Mike and their followers moved west. They entered the Mojave Desert west of their homes in Chemehuevi Valley to find a new home. They wanted to leave the fighting behind them and avoid their forced removal to the new reservation established primarily for Mojave in the Parker Valley.

 The two Mike brothers brought their families and other families from the Chemehuevi Valley into the Mojave Desert. They followed an ancient trail across the desert, always intending on stopping to rest at the Serrano village at the Oasis of Mara, a sacred place on the Salt Song Trail in eastern California. They looked forward to taking the water at the oasis, the plentiful water that bubbled up to the surface and formed ponds along the line of palm trees. The Mikes knew Serrano people would welcome them since they were old friends. At the oasis, the Chemehuevi could rest in the shade of the palm trees and enjoy the cool waters before moving on, continuing their journey to find a new home. From previous trips west to hunt, gather, and visit the Pacific Coast, Chemehuevi knew Serrano people. The Serrano had lived at the oasis since time immemorial. It was their origin place. The Oasis of Mara was the original settlement of the Desert Serrano who loved this special and powerful place on earth. Serrano had hunted, gathered, and raised a respectable garden. They had situated their village and garden on the north slope of the oasis, although some people lived in other areas along the tree line. For many years, the Serrano had a prosperous village at the oasis, but in the 1860s they abandoned their village, perhaps in response to a smallpox epidemic that swept through Southern California from the Pacific Coast into the inland deserts. Indian people living in the Mojave and Colorado Deserts experienced this horrific smallpox epidemic that originated in Los Angeles and traveled east to the Colorado River killing Chemehuevi, Mojave, Quechan, and Cocopa. The Serrano may have fled their village and retreated into the San Bernardino Mountains seeking refuge from the smallpox epidemic. When the epidemic subsided, they eventually returned to the oasis.

 When the Chemehuevi families first reached the Oasis of Mara, they found the village abandoned. Serrano houses stood empty. No one stirred. No dogs barked to announce their arrival. Everything was deathly quiet at the village, except for nearby calls of hawks, crows, doves, and quail. Chemehuevi elders ordered their people to make camp near the village but not disturb the Serrano lodges. At night the *Nuwuvi* people likely talked about the origins of the Serrano village. Surely someone knew the oral narrative about the first Serrano beings flying to the Oasis from Mara. According to contemporary Serrano elder Ernest Siva, Serrano descendants known as *Maarrenga'yam* floated to the oasis they called *Maarra'* after their former homeland. Their Lord, known as *Cheenep*, named the area for the Serrano, and proclaimed the area sacred, a powerful healing place. The place became known as the Oasis of Mara after their former homeland, and the site became their home. Chemehuevi travelers had heard this oral tradition, and they knew Mara meant Little Grass, Much Water. Over the course of many years, Serrano people had established a thriving village at the oasis in the middle of the Mojave Desert where they found an abundance of natural resources, especially water and productive soil. Whatever the cause, Serrano people had temporarily abandoned their village at the Oasis of Mara. When they returned later in the 1860s or 1870s, they found a band of Chemehuevi living at Twenty-Nine Palms.

After first arriving at the Oasis of Mara and finding the village abandoned, Jim Mike and his band decided to remain at the former Serrano village. Men and women likely discussed the matter and decided to remain at Mara because it was a good place to live. The site near a row of palm trees offered plenty of clean water, fertile soil, and seclusion from settlers. They liked the isolation, and they knew of the place from previous travels west to the Pacific Ocean and the San Bernardino Mountains where they had hunted and gathered. They decided to take advantage of a site they had known about since the origin of the Salt Songs, and they all had sung about the place during funerals when they sang death songs focused on the Salt Song Trail. Without taking over the abandoned houses, the Chemehuevi built their own homes and farmed the old Serrano garden. When the Serrano returned to the oasis, the two peoples agreed to live together. Perhaps some of the people knew each other from past visits, but for whatever reason the two groups agreed to share the village site, which had always been a Serrano site and their place of origin.

No records exist to describe what happened when the Serrano learned a band of Chemehuevi had settled near their village, but likely adult men and women from both tribes met in council to discuss matters. It was customary for the tribes to share food and tobacco at meetings, and often someone or a group sang and blew tobacco smoke in the four directions as a prayer. These ritual actions represented acts of peace and friendship, creating a spiritual bond between the two groups and a covenant connection with the Creator. Serrano elder Dorothy Ramon reported, "Chemehuevi men would talk" and "they spoke Serrano." The languages were not mutually intelligible, so they may have used interpreters and signs to seal the bond between the two tribes. In any case, the Serrano and Chemehuevi resolved to live next to each other in peace.

According to Dorothy Ramon, Jim Pine's father was Serrano and the *keeka* or tribal leader. When his father died, Jim Pine assumed the mantle of *keeka*, as his people looked to him as a caring and thoughtful leader, with healing power to boot. Pine's mother was Chemehuevi and may have known the Mike family before they resettled at the oasis. Pine grew up multilingual, speaking Serrano, Chemehuevi, and Spanish; he later learned English. Pine served as an interpreter for the people, an especially useful skill when the Serrano and Chemehuevi settled near the Oasis of Mara. Within a short time, the people living at the oasis village were intermarrying and referring to each other as brothers, sisters, aunts and uncles, fathers, mothers, grandfathers and grandmothers. From all accounts the people formed a community of mutual respect. At the same time, Chemehuevi and Serrano maintained their separate sacred ceremonial lodges overseen by the respective tribal elders. Intermarriage strengthened familial bonds between the two groups and they learned each other's songs, stories, ceremonies, and dances. Chemehuevi and Serrano considered Twenty-Nine

Palms "a great ceremonial site for Indians" where shamans erected two ceremonial houses, one for the Chemehuevi and one for the Serrano. It was not unusual for one tribe to attend ceremonies sponsored by the other, and they shared the medicine power offered by each group and the shaman living at the oasis.

Jim Pine (also known as *Akuuki* or Ancestor), Jim Mike, and William Mike lived together in peace, perhaps having known each other in years past. The leaders approached their relationship with each other and with the oasis in a spiritual manner, because of their shared belief that the oasis was a holy place. To the Serrano the oasis was the point of tribal origin, while from ancient times the Chemehuevi included the oasis as part of their great song cycle. The Oasis of Mara appears in the Chemehuevi Salt Songs and is part of the Salt Song Trail. Chemehuevi and Serrano people considered (and still consider) the oasis a holy site and sanctuary. This belief was rooted in the conviction that Twenty-Nine Palms contained spiritual power, drawing pilgrims to travel to the oasis for healing. William Mike and Jim Pine served Indian people through their own special songs, through which they called their familiars or spiritual helpers to come to them. Once a familiar arrived in spirit, the shaman took the familiar into their hands, received the power, and healed their patients. There were a number of reasons for Serrano and Chemehuevi considering the Oasis of Mara a healing place. The water offered healing power and on occasion shamans used the water from the oasis in their healing ceremonies. Dipping eagle feathers into ceramic bowls filled with water from the Oasis, shaman sprinkled it for purification on both living and dead. Serrano elder Dorothy Ramon remembered the oasis as a site "where shaman sang, conducted yearly renewal ceremonies, and held funerals and memorials."

During the first decade of the twentieth century, Jim Pine led the Serrano ceremonial lodge or "Big House" at the Oasis of Mara. Like the Chemehuevi, Serrano people believed the Creator spoke to the people through the Big House, giving instructions to ceremonial leaders for the benefit and protection of the people. Leaders then conveyed the wishes of the Creator to the people who acted on divine instructions. William Mike led the Chemehuevi ceremonial lodge and regularly healed people. All the tribes of Southern California believed in the power of the Big House and respected these lodges like Christians, Muslims, Maori, and Jews respect their places of worship. Native American and many newcomers consider the oasis at Twenty-Nine Palms to be a place of healing and renewal, and it remains a special spiritual place, particularly on the grounds of the 29 Palms Inn where the people had once established their village and garden.

Not long after settling at the Oasis of Mara, William Mike instructed his followers to build the Chemehuevi ceremonial house. As a result, the oasis contained two Big Houses where men and women met for ceremonies, wakes, memorials, and secular discussions about issues involving the entire village. The two ceremonial lodges served as a bond between the Serrano and Chemehuevi, as they both respected each other's beliefs, traditions, and ceremonies. The leaders shared in collective decision making whenever an issue involved the entire community. Women as well as men had a voice in the Big Houses. The people generally did not vote on matters, but they met to discuss important matters until they came to a consensus.

Chemehuevi and Serrano people worked out an economic relationship with each other, resulting in the Serrano hunting more than they had in the past. They hunted pronghorn, deer, bighorn sheep, tortoises, doves, ducks, quail, squirrels, wood rats, and rabbits. In the 1890s, *Chepeven*, a Chemehuevi centenarian, contributed to the Indian economy by hunting small game in the trees near the ponds at the oasis and sharing with his fellow residents. The Serrano had farmed a respectable garden on the north side of the oasis just east of the village for years, devising irrigation system using gravity to move the water from the slightly higher oasis and near the tree line to flow down a gradual slope to their crops. Chemehuevi expanded on this form of irrigation, clearing more land, creating irrigation ponds, and cultivating rows of crops. People from Chemehuevi Valley had a long and successful tradition of farming, and they put their skills to work at the Oasis of Mara. An abundance of reliable foods, including corn, beans, squash, melons, chilies, watermelon, and others was produced. To supplement their crops, Chemehuevi and Serrano gathered Native edibles, including yucca stalks and flowers, agave hearts, chia, cactus, mesquite beans, seeds, and acorns. Hunting and gathering over a vast desert area and in the Little San Bernardino and San Bernardino Mountains, the people at the Oasis of Mara enjoyed a healthy, well-balanced diet.

Before the 1850s, settlers, soldiers, and government agents knew little about the Oasis of Mara. In 1855, a commander of the United States Army instructed Colonel Henry Washington to survey the desert near the oasis. He called the palm trees "cabbage palmettos," but Professor H. Wendland named the indigenous palms, *Washingtonia filifera* after General George Washington, not the colonel. The next year, United States Government Surveyor A. P. Green made another reconnaissance of the oasis, reporting "some 26 fine large palm trees in Sec. 33 from which the springs take their name, Palm Springs." This was a misstatement, and no one after Green called the oasis Palm Springs. Native people referred to the village as the Oasis of Mara or Mara; later, the village came to be known as Twenty-Nine Palms.

The Oasis of Mara was rich in materials for creating useful and artistically designed items. Chemehuevi and Serrano women at the oasis gathered basketry materials together and sat for hours weaving beautiful baskets filled with wonderful, magical patterns. William Mike's wife, Maria, and her mother, Surda, distinguished themselves as world class basket makers. Other members of the community became famous for their works of art in diverse mediums. A Serrano elder named Allesandro drew fame for his rawhide bridles, ropes, reins, and other leather items used in wrangling horses and herding cattle. He also crafted intricate horsehair hatbands, bracelets, quirts, belts, and ropes. Although the village at Twenty-Nine Palms offered no market for Indian art, indigenous artists sold their baskets, beadwork, pottery, and other forms of art to merchants in Banning, Coachella, Indio, Palm Springs, San Bernardino, and other towns to sell to tourists, often traveling on trains and stagecoaches. They also sold their works to Indian traders. Cash earned from their handicrafts provided money to buy goods like coffee, flour, and sugar as well as any number of manufactured items: tools, nails, pots, pans, skillets, blankets, knives, axes, guns, ammunition, seeds, beads, blankets, cloth, clothing were all purchased by people at Twenty-Nine Palms. Such fiscal activity was typical as Native Americans joined the market economy.

By the time Willie Boy entered the village at Twenty-Nine Palms early in 1909, the Chemehuevi and Serrano had lived and worked side by side for over thirty years. Together, they had continued to practice their religions, maintained social relationships with themselves and others, preserved their tribal languages, and created an economy that worked well for them. In the early twentieth century, the Indian community at Twenty-Nine Palms used most of the water at the oasis, as they considered themselves the rightful "owners" of the land and surrounding water. Occasionally, newcomers filled their containers with fresh water from the oasis and watered their livestock as they passed through. Both Indian and non-Indian travelers used the oasis on their journeys, and villagers generously shared the water. No evidence exists that the Indians sold the water to travelers or that anyone paid for the water, including stage and freight companies driving their wooden wagons and modified stagecoaches called mud wagons through Twenty-Nine Palms.

As early as the 1860s, miners visited the area, prospecting the rugged rock and stony mountains surrounding the oasis for gold, silver, and other precious metals. Miners often frequented the Indian village at the oasis and used the water. They might stay a spell, but most non-Indians moved on after short stays. In 1873, a cattleman named Tom Coover brought cattle, horses, and sheep to the area to graze on the grass that once existed in the area. Other cowboys, including Indian cowboys, raised livestock at the oasis. Some tourists visited the Indian village and took in the awesome landscape of the desert and mountains surrounding the oasis. Now and then, health seekers appeared at Twenty-Nine Palms to take in the waters from the oasis or bathed in the springs as part of their health regimen. Health seekers also enjoyed the dry, warm climate. On one occasion, a freight driver named Pete Domac, a man of mixed Indian blood, brought a Mrs. Whallon and her daughter, Maria Eleanor Whallon, to the oasis in hope the waters and environment would save young Maria from tuberculosis. They camped at an old adobe building, but the young girl died the first night at the oasis and was buried nearby. In 1888, another health seeker named Reverend Halesworth visited the oasis hoping for a cure for his tuberculosis. Over the years other pilgrims sought medical relief at the Oasis of Mara.

One can empathize with a seriously ill individual or parent desperately searching for a cure to a deadly disease. Unfortunately, bacterial and viral infection posed a threat to the people of Twenty-Nine Palms, potentially exposing residents to devastating diseases, not least of all tuberculosis. No accounts were taken of Indian deaths caused by disease at the oasis, or even the degree of infections resulting from exposure to settlers. The lack of vital statistics on the health of either Indians or settlers means we can't accurately measure the impact of disease on Native Americans at the Oasis of Mara. The first census taken by the Indian Office of the Indians living at the Oasis of Mara came in the 1890s, though these early censuses are riddled with inaccuracies. But for a glimpse into the families and individuals living in the Indian village, the census material is valuable. It's the only information available about the first residents of the Indian village at the Oasis of Mara.

For insight into the people Willie Boy would have met when he entered the Indian village at Twenty-Nine Palms in 1909, the census names key individuals. Jim Pine led the desert Serrano of Twenty-Nine Palms. Born in 1840,

Jim was a member of the *Courinote* family but carried the English surname of Pine. His relatives called him *Akuuki*, meaning Ancestor, a name of high honor as it recognized his connection with past generations. Jim Pine gained a reputation as a great hunter, first with bow and arrows and, later, with a rifle. He was a natural leader, just as his father before him. Because his mother was Chemehuevi, Pine was raised with knowledge of her language and culture in a bicultural and bilingual home. As a member of a patrilineal society, Jim became a leader among his father's people and eventually the leader of the desert Serrano band at Twenty-Nine Palms and Mission Creek. In 1880, Jim Pine married Matilda and together they produced and buried a number of children at the oasis. With a lack of vital records, the causes of the children's deaths remain a mystery. Jim and Matilda laid their children to rest in the cemetery on Adobe Road in the present-day city of Twentynine Palms.

Chemehuevi Pancho Ramirez also lived at the oasis with his two children, Jacinta and Marcus, but the census makes no reference to Pancho's wife. Pancho contracted tuberculosis and died of the dreadful disease. The village included another man named Jacinto, his wife Carlota, and their son Berdugo, but nothing more is known of these people. One Joe Pacheco married Tomachi who was one of the daughters of Jim Mike, the headman and brother of William Mike, who had brought his people from Chemehuevi Valley to the Oasis of Mara. The couple had two sons, Harlie and John, and for many years the boys lived at the oasis until a job on the Baker and Shay Ranch took the family into Banning. Joe worked as an Indian cowboy riding for different outfits in the Banning Pass. Jim Mike also lived at Twenty-Nine Palms with his wife, Maria or Mary. A number of their children carried the surname of Mike, while others adopted the name Boniface. These children included Billy Mike, Minnie (also known as Annie), Lucy, Bob, and Jeff. Jim served as chief of the Chemehuevi at Twenty-Nine Palms until his death in 1903 when mourners buried him at the cemetery on Adobe Road. Following his death, his younger brother, William Mike, became the *Thau Winthum* or chief of the Twenty-Nine Palms Band of Chemehuevi Indians.

In the 1860s, Frank and Maria Holmes moved from the Chemehuevi Valley to the Oasis of Mara. It's unclear the exact number of children born to this couple, but one daughter named Nellie married Billy Mike, a son of Jim Mike. Nellie and Billy had two children, including Lucy and Mary. In the later nineteenth or early twentieth centuries, Nellie and Billy moved to Banning where Billy worked as a cowboy on various ranches. Their daughter Lucy moved with her parents to the Banning Pass where they lived on the Morongo Indian Reservation. Lucy became friends with the Cahuilla and Serrano Indians living on the Morongo Reservation. She first married Marcus Pete, then Joe Saubel. In 1909, the year Willie Boy settled at the village of Twenty-Nine Palms, Billy Mike died as a result of an accidental gunshot wound. While driving a wagon near Banning, California, a shotgun in the hold beside Billy accidentally discharged. Nellie later reported the front wheels of the wagon went over a bump, causing the gun to go off. The shotgun blast killed Billy Mike. During her time of mourning, Nellie moved back to the oasis for a spell in the aftermath of the tragic events involving William Mike, Willie Boy, and Carlota. Nellie Mike lived at the village of Twenty-Nine Palms until the Chemehuevi and Serrano abandoned their village in 1910. Nellie ultimately moved to the Banning Pass where she lived on the Morongo Indian Reservation, marrying Tom Morongo.

For many years, an elderly couple known as the Ticup or Waterman family lived at the village of Twenty-Nine Palms. Mr. and Mrs. Jim Ticup lived at the desert village. With a reputation as a dangerous man and superb hunter, Jim Ticup died in a hunting accident when a horse stumbled on a mountainside near Victorville. His widow remained at the oasis village to live with friends and family. Mrs. Ticup was, in fact, a key reason Willie Boy settled in the desert community: she was his grandmother. Besides the Ticups, Willie Boy had other relatives living at the oasis village, including his aunts and, at times, his mother, Mary Snyder (whose Indian name was *So Iris*). After his experiences in Victorville, Willie Boy opted to relocate to Twenty-Nine Palms and make the place his home among his extended family.

It was while living at the Oasis of Mara that Willie Boy met or was reintroduced to his cousin Carlota Mike. Chemehuevi tribal elders, including Mary Lou Brown and Alberta Van Fleet, maintained the couple were first cousins. Under *Nuwuvi* law, they were prohibited from marrying, so villagers and family members warned them against falling in love. Incest and marriage laws among Chemehuevi people prohibited the two from getting too close. Despite family warnings, the couple discounted the advice and refused to follow Chemehuevi protocols. Willie Boy and Carlota had to have known that William Mike was a conservative traditionalist who defended the ancient cultural laws of Chemehuevi people. Time-honored marriage laws held that couples must be a minimum of six generations apart in order to marry. It would have been no surprise that William Mike opposed their relationship because they were within the required degree of separation. Pursuing a romantic relationship was a serious violation of the tribe's spiritual laws.

As the Chemehuevi chief at the Oasis of Mara, William Mike held great sway over all matters affecting the village, including sanctioning marriages. William and his wife, Maria, had a number of children, including Little Mike (Lily), Jack, Sam, Albert, Johnson, Carlota, Susie, and Dorothy. Carlota was their oldest daughter, a beautiful and vivacious young woman with a delicate oval face, dark piercing eyes, and jet-black hair. According to the Mike family, she possessed a kind and generous demeanor, and she was patient with children, including her younger siblings. She charmed villagers and visitors to the oasis alike. In 1909, Carlota Mike was sixteen years old. Her life at that time revolved around helping her mother with her siblings and caring for other children living in the village. She was certainly no longer considered a child. At the age of eleven or twelve, she had completed her female puberty rites, which prepared her for womanhood in the Chemehuevi world. But while Carlota was old enough to marry, her culture required her to choose the correct man to become her husband; at the very least, the match must be approved.

In the tradition of Chemehuevi people, Carlota's parents sought a man worthy of their status to marry their daughter. William's elevated status as a tribal chief, shaman, and village leader mandated Carlota marry a man of equal or elevated standing, who was not too closely related and would be a good provider. Children in indigenous communities married the person their parents selected for them to marry; love, if it came, was an added bonus.

Regardless of these traditions in the Chemehuevi world, the times were changing in Indian Country, even within those villages far removed from settler communities. Young people wanted to decide for themselves who they would marry rather than wait for parental matchmaking. As of 1909, William and Maria Mike had not decided on a proper marriage partner for Carlota, or if they had, the arrangement had not been announced to other members of the family. But they hadn't relinquished the right to select Carlota's husband and fully intended to decide who and when she would wed. Carlota and Willie Boy had other plans.

Willie Boy, a natural athlete, played on an Indian baseball against white ballplayers in Victorville, California. A fight broke out and lawmen arrested the Indians, including Willie Boy, for disturbing the peace. This is his mug shot. Courtesy Harry Lawton Collection, Rivera Library, University of California, Riverside.

Chapter 3
The Love Affair

When Willie Boy joined the Chemehuevi community at the Oasis of Mara in 1909, there was little to foreshadow the calamity to come. It began with kinship, as Willie Boy and his two young wards sought family and stability at the oasis. There was the joy of reunion, the settling into new routines, and there was new love. Within a few months' time, death and heartache would wrench the community at its core.

It was natural for Willie Boy to turn to Twenty-Nine Palms following his troubles in Victorville. He'd previously visited the village where his grandparents and aunts lived alongside other relatives, including the family of William Mike. To one degree or the other, Willie Boy and members of the Mike family had kinship ties, though it's unclear how close Willie Boy was to the Mikes. Chemehuevi elders Alberta Van Fleet and Mary Lou Brown revealed to historians James Sandos and Larry Burgess that Willie Boy and Carlota were first cousins, but the depth of their friendship prior to Willie Boy's arrival at the oasis is uncertain.

Studying pictures taken of Willie Boy around this time provide little insight into the character of the man, or of his personality. His 1906 photo taken while in a San Bernardino County Jail is a haunting, black and white close-up of Willie Boy wearing jail-issued clothing. With tousled hair and strong features, it's apparent why Carlota would find him physically attractive. His mouth is slightly open, as if he is about to speak. But it's the eyes that capture your attention: what was he thinking as he gazed at the camera? Was he planning his future at the Oasis? Photographs often raise questions and create ambiguity; in this case, the photo of

Willie Boy fails to capture the full character, be it charm or intensity or humor, that led Carlota to risk so much for his love. And within a short time of Willie Boy's appearance at Twenty-Nine Palms, the two were very much in love.

According to Native American accounts, the couple wanted to marry despite their close degree of affinity. Every Indian person living at the village knew the incest laws of *Nuwuvi* people required the couple to be approximately six generations apart. From the outset of their relationship, Willie Boy and Carlota knew they should not marry, that such an act would violate Chemehuevi marriage and incest laws. But these two young people seemed less ingrained with conventional values, exposed as they were to influence from the "outside world" of white society. Traditional incest laws and cultural norms exerted less authority in 1909, at least where Willie Boy and Carlota were concerned.

Over the course of many years since 1909, Chemehuevi people have understood the story of Willie Boy and Carlota to be a tale of forbidden love. During an interview taken by historians James Sandos and Larry Burgess, Chemehuevi elder Mary Lou Brown explained the issue plainly: "one day he saw his cousin, Carlota, and he wanted her. She looked back at him openly." Chemehuevi beliefs forbade this love and the consequences for violating these norms extended beyond the couple. Breaking traditional marriage rules and violating tribal incest laws would affect every *Nuwuvi* person for all time. The covenant between the people and the Creator and between each other was one of group responsibility. Community members believed that any violation of tribal laws affected every other *Nuwuvi* person, not just at the oasis but among all Chemehuevi people generally. Tribal members at Twenty-Nine Palms publicly opposed the growing love affair between Willie Boy and Carlota. Anyone who sanctioned the relationship was just as guilty as the couple. Nonetheless, Carlota and Willie Boy willfully ignored tribal convention and the opposition from family and friends.

Carlota was just sixteen when she struck up a relationship with the twenty-eight-year-old Willie Boy. Indian Agent Clara True described Carlota as "physically a splendid specimen of Indian girlhood," and her elders had taught her "in the ways of her primitive people." True also claimed William Mike opposed the marriage "due to age differences." This was incorrect, though perhaps a more relatable interpretation from the white agent's perspective. Age was not an issue among the Chemehuevi because Carlota had already undergone her puberty ceremony. Older women had prayed for her and instructed her in the role of a Chemehuevi woman, wife, and mother in the traditional manner. Incest – as defined by Chemehuevi culture – was the issue. And as the daughter of a powerful tribal leader, Carlota was expected to set the bar for proper behavior. For many years Carlota had done just that, helping her mother and father raise their family, caring for the younger boys and girls. Most recently, Carlota had cared for her little sisters, Susie and baby Dorothy. Carlota was raised in a leadership family, with all the pressure and expectations that role entailed.

Indian Agent Clara True had met Carlota in May 1909 when the agent traveled with Pussyfoot Johnson to the Oasis of Mara to establish reservation boundaries for the Twenty-Nine Palms Band on their traditional homelands at the oasis. In her report to the Commissioner of Indian Affairs Robert Valentine, True noted that Willie Boy was "a good laborer." He dressed nicely and did not drink or gamble. Agent True's assessment of William Mike was also positive, crediting him as a devoted father and family man with a cheerful nature. Agent True also knew that when provoked, William Mike could be a dangerous man and certainly not someone to cross when serious cultural issues were at stake. Villagers must have been shocked when Carlota defied her father – and his leadership responsibilities – by seeking to marry her cousin. The resulting scandal was well-known to those living at the Oasis of Mara, and at the Serrano and Cahuilla communities in the surrounding area. Carlota broke from expectations and provoked an embarrassing confrontation with her father.

The conflict had its roots in the changing cultural and social environment of the early twentieth century. While William Mike was a traditionalist, Carlota and Willie Boy frequently interacted with people from other cultures. The reality of the world in which Carlota and Willie Boy came of age couldn't help but effect their own attitudes. White settlement forced tribal people to adjust to new social, cultural, and economic ways and while a challenge for all indigenous people, young people among the *Nuwuvi* of California, Great Basin, and the American Southwest would have felt the tug of western mores the most. Willie Boy and Carlota were no exception. During this time of great cultural change, it wasn't uncommon for young people to question the leadership of elders and traditional Chemehuevi practices. Certainly Willie Boy and Carlota interacted with non-Indians at villages, in towns, and on ranches. They were exposed, as previous generations had not been, to a new way of thinking and acting, including frontier traditions of couples falling in love and marrying without the permission of their parents. In fact, young people in settler communities did not wait for their elders to approve and arrange marriages, but followed their own feelings.

Willie Boy worked on ranches as a cowboy, learning to speak English and to shoot a rifle with great accuracy. He became a crack shot with a rifle, easily killing game animals many yards away. By all accounts, Carlota's congenial, outgoing personality served her well as cattlemen and miners living nearby came into the Oasis of Mara to visit and trade. The young woman interacted with settlers living in or near the oasis, and for many summers had traveled with her family into Banning to work at the Gilman Ranch. About a mile east of the Gilman Ranch was St. Boniface Indian School, where Carlota may have received some degree of formal education. Joseph Mike Benitez, grandson of William Mike, explained that people attached the name Boniface to the Mike family because some of the children of William and Maria Mike had attended the Saint Boniface Indian School in Banning. In the 1890s and early twentieth century, the school was a thriving off-reservation Indian boarding school sponsored by the Catholic Church and Office of Indian affairs. Although people referred to the family as Boniface, the family of William Mike had always adhered to the surname of Mike.

Like Carlota, Willie Boy had interacted with the rapidly changing world. At the same time, he was a follower of the Chemehuevi Ghost Dance religion, led by the Ghost Dance Prophet, Wovoka. Wovoka preached cooperation and friendship with white settlers, not violence, while also urging a return to Native values. *Nuwuvi* of the Chemehuevi Valley often sang and danced with their Hualapai neighbors at power sites where dancers found wild tobacco growing near panels of petroglyphs and pictographs. These were known places of *puha* or power. Chemehuevi people, especially young people, gravitated to the Ghost Dance because of the failure of traditional spiritual leaders to explain why creators such as Ocean Woman, Wolf, Coyote, Cougar, and others had allowed white encroachment, settlement of Indian lands, and theft of Indian resources. Many young Indians looked to their elder leaders to stop white influence on the lower Colorado River. But the old leadership and the old spiritual beliefs had failed to stem the tide of white settlement or government interference with Native American life. Willie Boy and other Chemehuevi applied the Ghost Dance to preserve and protect the indigenous ecosphere and ways of life. Ghost Dancers also sought to hasten the great apocalypse. Settlers would vanish and Indians could restore their spiritual balance and indigenous rights on earth without white influences. Ghost Dancers often danced near deposits of white clay, found near Chemehuevi Valley or present-day Havasu Landing, which they mixed with water and smeared on their hands and faces. The Ghost Dancers assumed a ghostly, other worldly appearance.

Tribal elders participating in the Ghost Dance ceremony purified the dance grounds, summoning power by blowing smoke in the four directions and enjoining the spirits to enter the ceremonial grounds. Previous to the opening ceremony, dance officials planted sticks marking the large circle where the people could perform. A large, sturdy pole often stood in the middle of the dance circle near the brightly glowing fire. As the ceremony opened, dance officials drew tribal elders to the middle of the dance circle as boys and girls, alternating boy-girl-boy-girl started the festivities. During the *Nikapi* ceremony, children danced first followed by adult participants. They danced the *Nikapi* or Circle Dance, much as we see today in Chemehuevi ceremony, but in both clockwise then counterclockwise directions. On occasion people swung their bodies around the center pole, falling to the ground in a trance. Willie Boy Ghost Danced to hasten the Indian apocalypse, which never occurred. It was an initial move away from the young Chemehuevi's traditional cultural ways. Conservative tribal elders, including William Mike, opposed the Ghost Dance movement and adhered to their traditional religions, refusing to accept Wovoka's teachings or participate in the Chemehuevi Ghost Dance.

In Ghost Dancing, Willie Boy drifted away from old cultural *Nuwuvi* ways, including adherence to traditional laws, opening the door to further break with his community's expectations. Willie Boy and Carlota willingly disregarded ancient tribal laws to pursue their own path as modern Indian people. They consciously embraced a new era of individual freedom, the "rugged individualism" Willie Boy came to appreciate through his work experiences within settler communities. "Modern" men and women, especially young people, made their own decisions and crafted their life choices without making allowance for ancient dogmas or communal structures. Willie Boy also witnessed greed and desire, traits that molded his approach to courting Carlota.

Most descendants of Carlota and Willie Boy's families don't speak about events surrounding the couple. Chemehuevi culture discourages them from speaking the names of the dead, and silence quiets their minds and their dreams. Only a few Chemehuevi elders have shared their knowledge about Willie Boy and Carlota, including Mary Lou Brown, Joe Mike Benitez, Adrian Fisher, Alberta Van Fleet, and Matthew Hanks Leivas. On February 15, 1991, Chemehuevi elder Mary Lou Brown told researchers James Sandos and Larry Burgess, "there's no point going into all this because, after all, they are gone, and we don't talk, we just don't talk about this once it's over." But Mary Lou Brown and other Chemehuevi elders did share their knowledge with two inquiring scholars, who reported as much in their original book, *The Hunt for Willie Boy*. Brown remembered her elders telling her that Willie Boy "needed a wife, but there were no young women nearby" in "Chemehuevi Valley" so "he went across the desert looking for a wife." According to all accounts from descendants of both families, Willie Boy and Carlota fell in love with each other and wanted to marry. This point – seen through the indigenous cultural lens of the Chemehuevi people – is critical in understanding the tragedy of Willie Boy and Carlota.

One night while Carlota herded her father's horses into a corral, Willie Boy proposed marriage and asked her to elope with him. That word – "elope" – indicates the couple understood their marriage would not be sanctioned in the traditional community. Quietly, at dusk, Carlota slipped away into the dark desert with Willie Boy. Planning to spend the rest of their lives together, they either didn't care about the reaction to their marriage and its wide-ranging consequences or were too much in love to have it matter. In eloping, they turned their backs on their upbringing and ran off to create a new world together. The impact of this decision can't be overstated: the couple ignored cultural laws, traditions, teachings, and permissions so fundamental to *Nuwuvi* people. Chemehuevi elder Alberta Van Fleet explained the burning desire felt by Willie Boy and Carlota to be together when the couple eloped. Van Fleet remembered elders telling her: "She wanted him. She wanted her way. He wanted his way. There had to be trouble, but the families didn't want it."

Chemehuevi elder Adrian Fisher told historians Larry Burgess and Jim Sandos: "People back then kept track of who were your relatives, who you could and could not marry. It seems strange now, we're all so intermingled." William Mike well understood tribal marriage laws, and a union between his daughter and Willie Boy was anathema. Everyone understood the two young people were too closely related to marry. William Mike expected his daughter and Willie Boy to honor the ancient laws of *Nuwuvi* people. For Chemehuevi people – indeed, all Southern Paiute people – Carlota and Willie Boy's actions constituted a serious cultural break with the laws of creation. The people believed in a covenant theology in which negative actions of one person or a few people could have damning consequences for many. Without giving their decision to marry the consideration it warranted under the circumstances, Willie Boy and Carlota invited tragedy, heartache, pain, and suffering into the lives of generations yet unborn.

Even today, the abhorrent behavior of the Willie Boy and Carlota remains an issue among Southern Paiute people, especially Chemehuevi. Their acts – in the least, irresponsible and at the worst, reprehensible – sticks in the craw of contemporary Chemehuevi and other Southern Paiute people. In the minds of the *Nuwuvi,* Chemehuevi people will carry the burden of Willie Boy and Carlota's marriage in violation of the old tribal laws throughout time. The Willie Boy story lives today within Native American communities, in part because of the cultural violations involved. Through spiritual law, every *Nuwuvi* person had the obligation to prevent such desecrations. If the people allowed the elopement and marriage of Willie Boy and Carlota to stand uncontested, all Southern Paiute people would forever bear the scar of this transgression. Contemporary Chemehuevi remember that Willie Boy and Carlota, "tried to do what was not right, what they should not have done." At the time they eloped, "they knew. She knew. He knew" they were violating sacred tribal commandments. Yet, Alberta Van Fleet explained, "they wanted it, but the families couldn't let it happen."

When William Mike's family and Willie Boy's family at the Oasis of Mara learned that Carlota and Willie Boy had eloped, they organized quickly to track down and bring the couple home. The families and other villagers joined in the hunt for the couple. At the time, Segundo Chino, a relative of Willie Boy and well-acquainted with both families, was visiting the village of Twenty-Nine Palms. Chino led the search for the couple. Today, many people believe Segundo Chino was a "Pass Cahuilla" or Serrano Indian. He identified as a Pass Cahuilla but he was also part Chemehuevi. According to *Nuwuvi* elder Larry Eddy, Segundo Chino "was one of us." Chemehuevi elder Van Fleet remarked that Chino "was from our family" and he "went to bring Willie Boy back the first time; it was his duty" as a Chemehuevi person who was related to Willie Boy. Even Segundo Chino felt the spiritual obligation to separate Carlota and Willie Boy because of their violation of cultural laws.

Since Willie Boy had broken tribal laws, Chino and members from each family as well as other villagers joined in the search for the couple. Family members "followed and found them" somewhere in the Mojave Desert. An experienced tracker, Chino led the search for Willie Boy and Carlota. He was largely responsible for finding the couple, causing a rift between Chino and Willie Boy. The search team brought Willie Boy and Carlota back to the oasis where tribal elders separated them, scolding Willie Boy for his unacceptable and (from the paternal point of view) perverse behavior, telling him "not to look at her again." Villagers, including his own relatives, banished Willie Boy from their oasis home. Separation, as they say, inevitably makes the heart grow fonder, at least when that separation is forced upon a couple in love. Mary Lou Brown added, "both of their hearts were still restless." Willie Boy's exile from the village at Twenty-Nine Palms did not deter his passion, for he "wanted Carlota, but her father was a man of power," and Willie Boy rightfully feared the older man. William Mike was in excellent shape physically, a former warrior, a shaman with spiritual powers and his message to Willie Boy was clear: stay away from Carlota and from Twenty-Nine Palms. Reluctantly and with more than a little resentment, Willie Boy left the oasis and drifted south into the Coachella Valley where he found work.

Following the exile of Willie Boy from the Oasis of Mara, the young man traveled into the Coachella Valley and eventually arrived in Banning, California, finding work on ranches and farms as well as with small businesses. He quickly earned a reputation as a productive worker, showing up for work on time and abstaining from alcohol. In the towns of the Coachella Valley, he found employment as a woodcutter, brick maker, cowboy, and hay bailer. Indian Agent Clara True verified that Willie Boy was always "well dressed," he "did not drink in any noticeable quantity and did not gamble", and he was a reliable laborer. In a newspaper article found in the *Morning Mission* and *Riverside Enterprise* on September 28, 1909, Riverside County Coroner Dickson reported: "Willie Boy was a hard-working Indian, and not addicted to drink." Dickson knew that Mr. Mike had told Willie Boy "to keep away from the tepee of 'Old Mike.' " In other words, Dickson knew that William Mike had warned Willie Boy to stay away from Carlota.

Once Willie Boy moved into Banning, he kept to himself and nurtured his ability to run like the wind. He moved from job to job, eventually finding work at the ranch where he lived in the bunkhouse with Arthur Gilman, not far from the family's beautiful ranch house, a Riverside County park today. By all reports before September 26, 1909, Willie Boy was an intelligent, affable young man who forged a friendship with Arthur Gilman and the Gilman family. Again, Willie Boy's more worthy characteristics surfaced. The Gilmans found him to be an excellent, sober, and reliable ranch hand. While Willie Boy made his way into new situations in Banning town, Carlota's life underwent new restrictions at Twenty-Nine Palms, as she moved into the home of her "uncle" and "auntie." In the home of Jim and Matilda Pine, Carlota was instructed in the proper behavior of a young *Nuwuvi* woman, in case a lack of training had led to her rebellious elopement. Maria Mike, Matilda Pine, Mrs. Ticup, and other *Nuwuvi* women then living at the oasis sought to impress on Carlota that a young, unmarried Chemehuevi woman owed her parents obedience, particularly on serious matters like marriage laws and sexual relations with her cousin. Carlota remained with the Pine family until the late spring of 1909 when her father and family began preparations to travel to, of all places, the Gilman Ranch for their summer employment.

Over the course of many years, William Mike had worked at the Gilman Ranch near Highland Springs just north of Banning. James Gilman bought the ranch in 1869 on land set not far from the San Andreas Fault. Evidence of the fault is apparent in the land rising up sharply into the San Bernardino Mountains, and in the San Gorgonio Pass in which Banning is situated. But the location of the ranch was due more to the open range and the three natural springs.

Each year the Gilman family hired William Mike as the Indian foreman and his people from the oasis to bring in summer crops. Late spring of 1909 was no different as William Mike and members of his family prepared to travel to the Gilman Ranch. The ranch hired Indian men, women, and children and while they didn't pay high wages, Chemehuevi workers used their wages to buy staples in town, which, with any luck, would last throughout the year. At the oasis, Indians found it hard to obtain basic supplies. With their earnings, a range of manufactured items could be obtained by the Chemehuevi: cooking utensils, clothing, cloth, coffee, sugar, flour, shoes, needles, saddles, blankets, bandanas, tools, guns, knives, axes, ammunition, hats, and a host of other trade goods. Banning merchants appreciated the local economic boon.

    The usual joy that accompanied preparations for their journey into Banning came to a sudden halt the evening before departure. From the south and west black clouds gathered over the Little San Bernardino Mountains above Twenty-Nine Palms. In the distance, villagers heard thunder rolling over the mountains as streaks of lightning animated the southern sky. The thunder grew ever louder as the mountains seemed to roar and the bright streaks of lightning traveled nearer to the village. Accompanying the drama of the thunderstorm, a driving rain emerged from the mountains but moved north toward the village.

    In the distance streaks of purple rain pounded the earth, filling nearby arroyos with rushing rainwater and bringing a torrent of flooding rainwater to the desert floor. The unremitting rains pounded the earth, racing down the mountain slopes toward the oasis and village of Twenty-Nine Palms. As the storm reached the oasis, sink holes opened and rainwater disappeared into a dark abyss below. For an already disquieted William Mike, the great storm was an omen warning him of impending doom. The shaman heard the voice of the mountain speaking to him: danger and death awaited him.

From the oasis at Twenty-Nine Palms, William Mike could not see Snow Mountain (*Navaganti*), the origin place of his people (known by whites as Mount Charleston in the Spring Mountains of Southern Nevada). To the south of Twenty-Nine Palms were the Little San Bernardino Mountains, William Mike's point of reference and the home of his familiar. This was, to William Mike, "my mountain": he followed deer and bighorn there, and spotted coyote, cougar, and bobcat, all sacred and spiritual animals to the Chemehuevi. He had no deed of ownership to the mountain, but his claim was based in a song describing the extent of the mountain range, the trails, caves, and places of water. Did William Mike's mountain contain immense *puha* or power? He believed it did. In those mountains William would sing, pray, and invite spiritual power to come into his mind and body, and the mountain spoke to him in response. White quartz came out of those mountains, stones containing spiritual power. Whenever a villager died, William and the people brought small chunks of white quartz down to the village to spread over the graves of loved ones. When a *Nuwuvi* living at the oasis was in need of healing, William Mike, as shaman or *puahgaant*, sang and prayed. Power came to him in the form of his familiar, a spirit animal or object bringing him his healing gift. The night before the Mike family left the oasis for Gilman Ranch, the mountain spoke to William Mike. The message was filled with foreboding – it forecast tragedy, danger, and doom.

A settler named William Sullivan visited the oasis at the time of the storm, and he wrote the commissioner of Indian affairs concerning the great storm and the effect it had on William Mike. According to Sullivan, William Mike confided in him that the voice of the mountain, through thunder, told him, "there would be some kind of tragedy to befall him or his family because of the roar from the mountain." Sullivan wrote, "fantastic and in our present day and age and life we're not supposed to believe in such things, they did and they really weren't surprised in any way of the tragic events which happened." In spite of the warning and premonition coming through the thunderous voice of the mountain, William Mike and his family began their journey to Banning.

William Mike heard the spirits and was resigned to his unalterable fate, whatever it might be. Destiny led him and his family down the path before them leading to Gilman Ranch and summer work in the cooler climate of the Banning Pass. Each year, the family pitched their tent under giant cottonwood trees east of the Gilman's ranch house and not far from olive, plum, peach, and apricot trees that moderated temperatures at the ranch. A breeze often blew through the Gilman Ranch, providing relief from the blazing summer sun. Without a specific and detailed premonition, there was no justification for not continuing with the annual trek, but spiritual forces, the people say, predetermined William Mike's future. He stoically told Sullivan no one could change his destiny or the course of events. Indian families planning to journey to the Banning Pass rounded up their horses, greased their wagon wheels, filled barrels with water, and prepared harnesses for their teams. Women and girls packed food, bedding, water, tents and tools for their impending move across the Mojave Desert.

Carlota and her brothers prepared the family for days of travel. William, Maria, and their Mike children as well as William's nephew, Billy Mike, his wife, Nellie, and the other families gathered their belongings. Soon the little caravan of Indians began their trek across the Mojave Desert. Mrs. Ticup, her sisters, and other tribal elders remained at the oasis to watch over the village, making baskets and gathering foods for the upcoming year. Mary Snyder, Willie Boy's mother, also remained at the village.

Chemehuevi families always looked forward to spending the summer at the Gilman Ranch in the Banning Pass. The foothills of the San Bernardino Mountains offered them a chance to live, work, and sleep in cooler climes. At Gilman Ranch, the families could be together on a working vacation where they camped in the shade of trees lining a small babbling stream. The fruit and olive trees lining the ranch offered the Mike family a change in diet, full of fresh fruit that Maria, Carlota, and Nellie prepared in a variety of ways. At night, Indian workers found respite from the burning sun, especially when a cool breeze blew through the green leaves bringing a Pacific wind. While the families toiled in the sun preparing for their trip to the Banning Pass, the effort was less onerous when thinking of their destination and the pleasure they would find at the Gilman Ranch.

The Mike family included William's daughters Carlota, Susie, and Dorothy; his sons included Lily (Little), Jack, Sam, Albert, and Johnson. At least some of William's children loaded the family wagon for the trip from the high desert to the low desert. When William and the other Chemehuevi pulled out from the oasis, they said goodbye to Mrs. Ticup and her two sisters as well as *So Iris*, better known by her English name, Mary Snyder. Willie Boy's mother was living at the village at Twenty-Nine Palms at the time, but only a few people outside of the Indian community knew her identity, certainly not the county sheriffs or their deputies. From the Oasis of Mara, William Mike's band traveled due west of the oasis, following the old Indian trail that ran along the face of the mountains to their immediate left. The trail gradually turned south at the present-day town of Joshua Tree, California.

William's wagon train carefully avoided the soft sand that could bog down the wagons and impede their progress. William led the caravan, directing his people to drive their wagon teams through rocky ground along a well-worn trail so their broad wooden wheels would not sink into the desert sand. The Little San Bernardino Mountains rose rapidly in rugged relief against the deep blue sky. The sun animated the mountains, casting shadows that produced ever-changing colors on the dark rugged rocks. From the trail, the travelers could see for miles in all directions. To the southwest, the Chemehuevi saw the great San Gorgonio Peak that at times displayed traces of snow on its northern slopes. The desert to the north opened up into a wide, hilly desert that sloped downward into the sandy basin of dry lakebeds. Periodically the people watched dust devils whirl across the desert, which concerned and unnerved them. *Nuwuvi* people disliked dust devils, which they believed carried dangerous spirits. If a whirlwind approached them, they chased the wind with brooms, switches, sticks, or whatever tools they had on hand to beat down the wind and drive away the evil contained within the whirling wind.

At the present-day site of Yucca Valley, a town that did not exist at the time, the Chemehuevi turned their teams south, following a steep mountain trail some distance before entering a gentle valley known as the Morongo Basin. From the valley below, the teams traveled a circuitous route down another steep grade through Big Morongo Canyon, arriving in the mountainous and sandy foothills of the western edge of the Coachella Valley and the Colorado Desert. The small wagon train turned northwest, up another long grade past the Whitewater River where they stopped briefly to rest. At Whitewater, they allowed their teams to drink cold pure water rushing down from the San Bernardino Mountains. The Chemehuevi camped on the Whitewater River north of Palm Springs, allowing the people and their livestock to rest and enjoy the rushing river water. Children played in the shallow but freezing waters of the Whitewater River, refreshing themselves in innocent play. They waded in the water over the smooth round rocks and camped on the gravel and sandy banks of the river.

 At this special spot, the water rushed over the rocks in great ripples. The older young people like Carlota watched over the smaller children, while the parents prepared for the last stretch of their journey up the hill through the Banning Pass. At Whitewater, the people camped in the shadow of two sacred mountains that watched over the pass like two giant sentinels. Mount San Jacinto rose up to the south and faced the greater Mount San Gorgonio to the north. Both mountains called the clouds to their peaks to provide moisture for the thirsty deserts and valleys below. Mount San Jacinto reached 10,333 feet and Mount San Gorgonio climbed to 11,503 feet high, each guarding the Banning Pass, and many indigenous people considered them places of power and danger. Chemehuevi, Cahuilla, Serrano, Quechan and other Native Americans considered these mountain holy places. For many tribes, a god named *Tahquitz* lived on

Mount San Jacinto and had made the mountain his home since the time of creation. *Tahquitz* was a dangerous spirit. Contemporary Cahuilla people, including Sean Milanovich and Alvino Siva, have reported seeing the spirit. Many other Indians believe *Tahquitz* remains in his domain today and throughout time.

From the Chemehuevi camp on the Whitewater River, William Mike's caravan traveled west up a steep grade through the Banning Pass. It's easy to imagine the excitement as Mr. Mike moved his entire band northwest to Banning in the shadow of the mountains. A change of pace, rekindling old friendships, and earning cash to buy useful goods awaited the band from Twenty-Nine Palms. The Gilman family always greeted the Indian families personally, reflecting the strong friendship built over years of interaction. William Mike directed his people to unload the wagons and make camp, dividing chores among his group. Some of his party pitched a tent in the ravine east of the ranch house, while others unhitched the horses from the wagon, removed their harnesses, and currycombed the horses. The animals were watered and fed. Still others gathered wood and started a small fire for cooking and an ambient light for the evening, taking care to keep the fire at a minimal level. The Mike family and other Chemehuevi settled into a peaceful place in the shade of a cottonwood grove, preparing to begin work the following morning.

As the Indian foreman for the ranch, it was William Mike's responsibility to set up crews of people to work in various areas of the ranch. Those who had worked well together in previous seasons were assigned to crews, often grouped according to tribes speaking the same language for easy communication. William's fluency in Chemehuevi,

Serrano, Cahuilla, and English allowed him to communicate work assignments to each crew, though at times he relied on interpreters speaking Spanish. William primarily supervised the Indian crews, but also helped the Gilman family provide guidance and instructions to others working at the ranch. Mike had his crews thinning, picking, pruning, and drying soft fruit. He had some crews cutting weeds, watering, and generally caring for fruit trees. Other crews worked in the olive groves, most of which the Gilman family pressed into olive oil. Everyone in William's family worked, including Maria who was nursing baby Dorothy.

When asked to help out with the animals, William Mike and his crew cleaned stalls, removing animal waste the Gilman family used for fertilizer. Indian workers fed livestock, especially in preparation for fall butchering. Gilman Ranch could be an interesting place to work, each day a little different than the one before. The Gilman family remembered the Mike family members as hard working ranch hands, including Mike's wife, Maria, and their older children. During the summer of 1909, William's oldest daughter, Carlota, also worked with the family on the Gilman Ranch under the direction of her father. Much was expected of Carlota, both as the oldest girl and because of her recent escapade with Willie Boy.

During the summer of 1909, the Gilman family also hired Willie Boy. They had heard from other employers that Willie Boy was a good worker and never drank. He always showed up to work on time and sober. The Gilman family knew little or nothing of events that had transpired at the Oasis of Mara where Willie Boy had eloped with Carlota only to be separated by family members. That was Indian business that remained within the Native American communities.

Had Willie Boy heard Carlota was working at Gilman Ranch? Would she have risked telling him where she would be that summer? Whether he came for work or for Carlota, almost immediately after Willie Boy arrived at the ranch, the two made it a point to flirt whenever they had a chance. Tribal elders say, Willie Boy and Carlota "made eyes at each other." No one knows exactly what was said between the two, although later events indicate they discussed eloping again. This time they would have to travel far away, safe from discovery by either Carlota's family or Willie Boy's family. Carlota was unwilling to take such a drastic step. According to tribal elders, Carlota insisted on obtaining her father's permission to marry, though Willie Boy and Carlota already knew William Mike's position: he opposed the match because they were too closely related.

It's an indication of the depths of Willie Boy's feelings for Carlota that he agreed to speak to William Mike, for he greatly feared the spiritual and physical power of the man. For her part, Carlota wanted to marry Willie Boy, but she loathed disappointing her father and violating Chemehuevi law. A young girl in love, Carlota found herself torn between her love for Willie Boy and her respect for her father and his values. It was an impossible situation. William wanted his daughter to follow tribal law, which would have prevented the couple from marrying and settling alongside their families. According to tribal elder Alberta Van Fleet, a relative of Willie Boy, "if they had stayed together, both families would have cut them off." With the hope and optimism (some might say naiveté) of a young couple in love, they clung to the hope that if Willie Boy could just talk to William Mike, the elder would come around to their point of view. At the core of this miscalculation is the fact that more was at stake than a couple in love; this involved a clash between Chemehuevi mores and the couple's desire to follow a new path, reflecting a modern course heavily influenced by the individualism of western society.

Although reluctant to cut off family ties, Carlota seemed willing to marry Willie Boy in violation of tribal law, but only if her father gave his approval or refused to say anything about the match, which was a cultural way for indigenous people to say no. There is no doubt that feelings between Willie Boy and Carlota ran deep, and that Willie Boy desperately wanted to be with Carlota, a woman Mary Lou Brown called "his wife." Contemporary tribal elders feel that genuine love existed between the couple. So, when Carlota insisted Willie Boy speak to her father one last time, the young man agreed, though he feared a confrontation with William Mike. Intimidated by the 65-year-old leader and knowing that William Mike could cause real harm – physical or metaphysical – Willie Boy carried a loaded rifle with him as he walked into William Mike's large canvas tent. No doubt, Willie Boy feared the *puahgaant*, the shaman, and the *Thau Winthum* or chief of the Twenty-Nine Palms Band of Chemehuevi Indians.

Willie Boy might have been frightened at the prospect of meeting his future father-in-law, or perhaps he anticipated an altercation when he put forth his case to marry Carlota. At any rate, sometime around 9 p.m. Willie Boy took possession of a .30-30 caliber rifle, loaded with cartridges, belonging to his friend Arthur Gilman – a gun to balance the innate power of the tribal chief. In what may have felt like an eternity, Willie Boy carried the gun across the ranch grounds, past the house and workshops to the small creek beside the large tent where William was preparing for the evening. Gauging intent is always an imprecise art, and interpretations of Willie Boy's plans vary according to the sources being examined. Native Americans claim Willie Boy did not plot to murder his future father-in-law on Sunday night, September 26, 1909, when he walked into the elder's tent. Reportedly, the two men fought. William Mike's grandson, Joe Mike Benitez, provided the family's interpretation of what happened when Willie Boy met William Mike. Joe's mother, Susie Mike, told her son that her father and Willie Boy struggled for control of the gun and it went off. Afterwards, the couple left the ranch, taking a few supplies before they left, including Willie boy's famous leather coat, a skin filled with water, a rifle, and additional shells for the .30-30.

The question, then and now, is what exactly happened during the brief meeting between the father and his daughter's young lover. Was this a cold-blooded murder? An argument gone wrong? Or as Joe Benitez explained, a struggle for the control of the rifle? No one can say for certain whether Willie Boy killed William Mike in cold calculation, or accidentally in the struggle for the gun. But a feasible argument can be made along the following lines: William Mike and tribal elders from both families believed they had permanently ended the relationship between Carlota and Willie Boy when the couple tried to elope earlier. Willie Boy caught William Mike unaware when he entered the tent that Sunday night seeking William Mike's blessing. The proposal likely angered the older man and during an undoubtedly heated confrontation, Native Americans claim that William Mike grabbed the barrel of the rifle.

Opinions crystallized rapidly following the killing. Many accounts surfaced in the aftermath of William's death, especially newspaper write-ups. Reporters and others described the killing as if they were eyewitnesses to the tragic event, but no one else saw the interaction between the men. These accounts are conjecture, manufactured in an era of yellow journalism where newspapers played loose with the facts to sell papers. Native accounts reflect knowledge from those who, though not in the tent, personally knew the participants in the tragedy and their background story.

Indians claim Willie Boy had no intention of killing William Mike, though he approached the tribal leader with trepidation. Carrying the gun was more about bolstering Willie Boy's confidence than anything else. In 1991, Chemehuevi elder Mary Lou Brown shared her version of the story very succinctly, saying, "One night Willie Boy got a rifle and came to see her father. They argued, and Willie Boy got mad. Willie killed her father." Most Chemehuevi say that Willie Boy did not murder Mr. Mike in cold blood. Chemehuevi historian and singer Matthew Hanks Leivas said the men fought over the gun. As the two men fought over control of the weapon, the gun went off into William's eye, exiting the top of his head. Forensic evidence doesn't dispute the Native interpretation: William had gunpowder burns on his face, and the trajectory of the bullet indicated that Willie Boy shot William at very close range. William Mike immediately fell to the ground, and his family found him dead in a pool of blood and brains.

The lack of eyewitnesses has led speculation to run rampant over the years. With little or no evidence, only conjecture, people recorded their version of the killing of Mr. Mike. From the aftermath in 1909 through the mid-20th century, a handful of writers spun a lurid tale as if reporting facts, including journalists and fiction writers. Without verification several newspaper writers claimed Willie Boy ambushed William Mike and shot the chief while he was sleeping. The gunshot, these authors claimed, must have awakened the Mike family and other workers camped under the stars that September night. The authors continued to claim that with his rifle in hand, Willie quickly realized the severity of his actions, and he moved swiftly to find Carlota and leave the area. Ethel Gilman estimated that Willie took fifty cartridges before he fled. He may have taken more or less.

Willie Boy wanted Carlota to run away with him, and she did. Non-Indians claimed Willie Boy threatened the entire Mike family with the gun, saying he would kill anyone that tried to stop the couple from leaving or if they tried to follow them. Indian voices dispute this characterization, though the chaos of events created pandemonium, grief, and fear. After Willie Boy and Carlota fled the ranch, Maria reportedly took her children into the steep dark hills above the Gilman Ranch where they spent the night in fear. The police were notified the following morning, either by Maria or one of the older children. The Indian police on the Morongo Indian Reservation were first contacted, specifically Segundo Chino. The Gilman family alerted Riverside County Sheriff deputies in Banning the morning after the shooting, which brought the county lawmen into the picture. As for Willie Boy, he took Carlota and ran southeast toward Whitewater. Chemehuevi elder Mary Lou Brown explained that after Willie Boy killed William Mike, "he and Carlota ran away again," meaning this was the second time the couple broke tribal law and eloped. Certainly, circumstances were much different this time. Willie Boy had killed Mr. Mike and lawmen were now involved. Mary Lou Brown made this assessment of the situation, saying, "Willie Boy came to Mr. Mike . . . and they argued. But

Willie Boy brought a gun. He never should have killed Mr. Mike 'cause there was no going back then, not like before."

There was never any going back for anyone. True – the voice of the mountain had foreshadowed the tragedy befalling William Mike, but his death was just the beginning of multiple miseries for the families of William Mike, Willie Boy, and *Nuwuvi* people generally. There is the death of William Mike, of course, but for the families of Carlota and Willie Boy the popularization of their families' story is painful. Willie Boy has been depicted as crazy, a drinker, a rapist and a cold-blooded murderer; at the same time, people have made heroes of the posse members and the lawmen who chased Willie Boy and Carlota. Most writers have no way of knowing the Indian story or its impact on Chemehuevi families involved, but their perspective is valuable and worth considering. Willie Boy's family lives with the fact that their relative killed a good and honorable Chemehuevi man, and his actions ultimately led to two additional deaths. Over the past century, the two families have come to an understanding with each other: while setting aside the painful cultural violations, the memory of Willie Boy and Carlota lingers. Descendants of William Mike and Willie Boy remain reluctant to talk about the events, not out of shame but of a taboo regarding speaking about the dead. Thankfully some contemporary Chemehuevi have shared their knowledge of the Willie Boy affair, providing greater insight and less speculation than found in earlier accounts. Chemehuevi elders admit that Carlota went with Willie Boy willingly and that Willie did not kidnap her or force her leave her family. Though grief-stricken over losing her father at the hands of the man she loved, Carlota nevertheless ran off with Willie Boy on her own volition, not at the point of a gun. According to one member of the posse, Carlota worked with Willie Boy in an attempt to hide their tracks as they fled into the foothills of the San Bernardino Mountains.

In their accounts about Willie Boy, William Mike, and Carlota Mike, Chemehuevi and Southern Paiute people accept that Willie Boy committed a selfish and purposeful act of violence. Killing Mike was, for Chemehuevi people, an unthinkable aggression against a fellow Chemehuevi and notable leader. Willie Boy's murder of Mr. Mike constituted a violation of *Nuwuvi* law, whether the shooting of Mr. Mike was an accident or not. Because of his rash behavior Willie Boy placed himself in jeopardy with the spirit world and all *Nuwuvi* people: he knowingly took a gun when he visited William Mike to discuss the couple's desire to marry. Under tribal law, the killing of another *Nuwuvi* was a heinous crime. The act of killing another member of the larger group of Southern Paiute people proved an assault on traditional norms that affected *Nuwuvi* people, families, and tribes. Willie Boy's act still resonates with Southern Paiute people. While they are loathe to revisit the topic, details have been handed down through the years, including the family's assessment of what happened in the fall of 1909.

Among the Southern Paiute, Willie Boy's offense occurred on several counts. First, his actions impacted not just himself and Carlota, but rippled throughout the community at Twenty-Nine Palms and beyond. A dark cloud had, according to tribal tradition, been created over every person within every band and for all times. His violation of tribal laws was that significant. Second, Willie Boy acted out of self-interests, allowing his desire for Carlota to overshadow his obligation to follow cultural norms of his larger community. Third, Carlota shared in the blame, flirting with him and encouraging Willie Boy to pursue her. She was young and smitten with the older, more experienced man. But even when confronted and returned from the elopement, she continued to disobey her parents, aunts, and uncles. Her infatuation led her to choose Willie Boy over tribal custom, plunging her family and the tribe into a state of violence and imbalance. Her desire made her complicit in the actions of Willie Boy. In the eyes of Chemehuevi people, she was culpable and not a victim of Willie Boy's injurious actions.

Chemehuevi elder Mary Lou Brown explained that throughout her life, her own mother mentioned the awful events surrounding the entire Willie Boy saga, saying, "Whenever my mother would tell this story, she always began by saying: 'Love is hard.'" Mary Lou's mother "would shake her head and say, 'Love is hard.' What she meant was that love should never have happened. Never." In the past, Chemehuevi elders rarely spoke of the events surrounding the deaths brought on by Willie Boy's and Carlota's actions. But in the last decade of the century in which the Willie Boy saga took place, some of those elders opened up to Professors Larry Burgess and James Sandos. It was a striking investment of trust in the two scholars in offering their interpretation of events, centered on tribal laws. Tribal elders on the Colorado River Indian Reservation and Cabazon Indian Reservation emphasized the couple's overt breach of cultural norms. Of course, strict tribal marriage rules gradually broke down with time, but in 1909 tribal elders vigorously and diligently enforced incest laws. They took these measures very seriously. While the families tried to check the couple's desire through lectures, separation, and strict instruction, their failure to finish the romance led to death and the Great Western Manhunt.

Willie Boy, the only known picture of the Chemehuevi Runner where he posed for a photograph. He is known in Indian Country as the man that outsmarted lawmen and lived to see another day. Courtesy Harry Lawton Collection, Rivera Library, University of California, Riverside.

In the late spring 1909, William Mike brought his family and other Chemehuevi to Banning, California, to work on the Gilman Ranch. This is a picture of the main street running through Banning. The posse that chased Willie Boy and Carlota launched their expeditions into the Mojave Desert from Banning. Courtesy Harry Lawton Collection, Rivera Library, University of California, Riverside.

Frank Wilson was Sheriff of Riverside County and ordered the posse to begin the hunt for Willie Boy in September 1909. John Ralphs, Sheriff of San Bernardino County, and Wilson were heavily involved in the chase to find and kill Willie Boy, but both lawmen failed to capture or kill Willie Boy. Courtesy Harry Lawton Collection, Rivera Library, University of California, Riverside.

After Willie Boy accidently shot and killed William Mike, Sheriff Wilson ordered the production of this wanted poster, offering a $50 reward and providing a brief description of the Indian outlaw. Courtesy Harry Lawton Collection, Rivera Library, University of California, Riverside.

Riverside, Cal., Oct. 1st, 1909

Wanted for Murder
$50.00 Reward

Willie Boy, a Chimawawa Indian. 28 years old. Height 5 feet 8 or 9 inches. Weight 150 pounds. Smooth face. Medium build. Has a scar under his chin where he was shot about three years ago, the bullet coming out of the mouth, taking out two or three teeth. Wore new black hat, dark gray coat and pants.

Willie Boy is wanted for the murder of Old Mike, an Indian, on Sept. 26, 1909, at Banning, Cal. He also shot and killed Old Mike's daughter on Sept. 30th, after forcing her to follow him 70 miles in the mountains. He was trailed to a point about 25 miles northeast of The Pipes in the San Bernardino mountains on Sept. 30, 1909, and was headed toward Daggett or Newberry. He has a 30-30 rifle with him and is a desperate man. Take no chances with him. I hold warrant for murder. Arrest and send any information to

F. P. WILSON, Sheriff.

As the posse closed in on Willie Boy and Carlota at The Pipes, Willie Boy left the area to secure food, leaving Carlota to rest. Indian trackers mistook Carlota for Willie Boy and accidentally shot her. The posse blamed Carlota's death on Willie Boy and issued a new Wanted Poster for a "Double Murderer." The lawmen pinned Carlota's death on the Indian outlaw, Willie Boy. Courtesy Harry Lawton Collection, Rivera Library, University of California, Riverside.

Arrest for Double Murder

San Bernardino, Cal., Oct. 5, 1909

Willie Boy

A Chimehuevis Indian, 26 years old, about 5 feet, 10 inches in height; slim built, walks and stands erect; yellowish complexion, sunken cheeks; high cheek bones; talks good English with a drawl; has a scar under chin where he has been shot and some teeth gone. For years lived about Victorville, with a halfbreed American woman with two children, a girl of 10 and a boy of 2 years. She left him because he had beaten her, and returned to Victorville. His people living among the Kingston mountains, along the Nevada state line. He killed Mike Boniface, at Banning on the night of Sunday, September 26, and Ioleta Boniface, at The Pipes, in San Bernardino county, September 30.

An Indian filling the description of Willie Boy was seen cooking a rabbit between Goffs Station and Manvel on Sunday evening, October 3rd. When he saw the approaching parties he ran away. This might have been Willie Boy as his mother was at Vanderbilt a short time ago.

J. C. RALPHS, Sheriff.

Found dead Oct. 15-09.

Segundo Chino was a well-known Indian policeman on the Morongo Indian Reservation. He was a Pass Cahuilla with Chemehuevi blood. He was related to Willie Boy's family and helped the posse chase Willie Boy. Courtesy Harry Lawton Collection, Rivera Library, University of California, Riverside.

One of the most famous posse members, Ben de Crevecoeur, was well known as a storyteller. He took great pleasure providing newspaper editors unsubstantiated stories about the early expeditions against Willie Boy, often embellishing or stretching his accounts that Carlota left pictographs indicating Willie Boy beat and raped her. Courtesy Harry Lawton Collection, Rivera Library, University of California, Riverside.

Ben's brother Wal de Crevecoeur participated on the Sheriff's posse, chasing Willie Boy. Randolph Madison had a camera and took many staged pictures of the posse. Courtesy Harry Lawton Collection, Rivera Library, University of California, Riverside.

Joe Knowlin posed for this photograph before leaving Banning for the Mojave Desert in pursuit of Willie Boy and Carlota. Like all the lawmen, he was well armed with a rifle and six gun. Courtesy Harry Lawton Collection, Rivera Library, University of California, Riverside.

Newspaper man turned deputy sheriff, Randolph Madison mounted up to chase Willie Boy. He joined the posse in October 1909 during the final journey into the Mojave Desert. He failed to take a candid closeup photograph of the man's face before the posse placed a black cloth on the face of the man lying on the ground. Courtesy Harry Lawton Collection, Rivera Library, University of California, Riverside.

This is a closeup of Randolph Madison in front of the *Los Angeles Record* newspaper offices. The relative of President James Madison was an accomplished writer of yellow journalism, which helped sell newspapers but little accuracy or truth. Courtesy Harry Lawton Collection, Rivera Library, University of California, Riverside.

Deputy Sheriff Charlie Reche led the posse to Ruby Mountain where Willie Boy ambushed and accidentally shot Reche in the hip. Reche survived a serious bullet wound, and in 1910, Madison took this photograph of Charlie. Courtesy Harry Lawton Collection, Rivera Library, University of California, Riverside.

Clara True served as Indian Agent of the Malki Agency, one part of the Mission Indian Agency. She was one of the few women to serve as an Indian agent, and she generally had a positive relationship with Indian people. Her report on Willie Boy is filled with errors and assumptions. Courtesy Harry Lawton Collection, Rivera Library, University of California, Riverside.

Not long before Willie Boy killed Mr. Mike, Clara True traveled to the Oasis of Mara to survey a reservation home for the people living at Twenty-Nine Palms. After filing this reservation with the United States Land Commission, she learned that the state first claimed the Indian land without permission or consultation. The state sold their title of the Oasis of Mara to the Southern Pacific Railroad. Neither the United State nor California had a "legal" relationship with Serrano and Chemehuevi of the oasis, which made it easier for the nation and state to steal Indian lands at the oasis. Courtesy Harry Lawton Collection, Rivera Library, University of California, Riverside.

After the deaths of William Mike and his daughter, Carlota, Riverside County Sheriff Wilson turned the bodies over to Maria Mike. She asked Serrano Indians on the Morongo Reservation to host wakes for William and Carlota at the Serrano Big House. The Indians sang death songs in the Big House shown here, sending father and daughter to *Nuva Kiav*, the hole in the sky near Mount Charleston. Courtesy Harry Lawton Collection, Rivera Library, University of California, Riverside.

This photograph shows the posse's supply wagon traveling over the rocks at the Whitewater River where the posse rested before turning north through mountain passes on their way to the Mojave Desert. Courtesy Harry Lawton Collection, Rivera Library, University of California, Riverside.

In the area near present-day Yucca Valley, the posse dismounted to look for Willie Boy's tracks in the desert sand. Courtesy Harry Lawton Collection, Rivera Library, University of California, Riverside.

On their last trip into the Mojave Desert, the posse claimed they found Willie Boy dead, lying in the shadow of a rock. The posse placed a black cloth over the man's face and took no pictures of the person's face. The posse failed to cut off this man's head as proof they had found Willie Boy dead. Courtesy Harry Lawton Collection, Rivera Library, University of California, Riverside.

This is a closer view of the large body on the ground. The posse failed to make a definite identification of the "body" with a black cloth over the face. This purported photograph of Willie Boy runs contrary to photographs taken of dead outlaws of the American West, shot to prove that lawmen got their man. Courtesy Harry Lawton Collection, Rivera Library, University of California, Riverside.

Chapter 4
Losing Carlota

    The morning after William's death, Maria Mike and her children returned from the Morongo Hills to inform lawmen of the killing. At 9 a.m. on September 27, 1909, Maria Mike reported the death of her husband to the Indian police on the Morongo Indian Reservation, about the same time that the Gilmans contacted the Riverside County Sheriff's Department to report the murder. The Indian police referred the information to Riverside County Sheriff Frank Wilson. The news spread like wildfire as deputy sheriffs and the public learned various versions of the truth. The core facts remained the same – that Willie Boy had shot William Mike at point blank range, killing the old man. Almost immediately newspaper reporters swarmed around the Gilman Ranch. Lurid stories were conjured up to sell more newspapers, not bothering to corroborate facts or undertake basic research, all too common for news reporting in the early 20th century. The same day Maria Mike reported the murder, one newspaper announced: "Mike Boniface, a well-known Banning Indian, was shot and instantly killed last night at 9'oclock by a young Indian known as 'Billy Boy.'"

    The errors in this reporting goes to the most basic facts: William Mike was misidentified as Boniface and Willie Boy as Billy Boy. No one, not Indian people or the whites he'd worked for called Willie Boy by the name Billy Boy. But the press loved the alliteration and often replicated the error. Another factual mistake centered on Carlota and served to portray Willie Boy as a deviant as well as a murder. After the death of Mr. Mike, the reporter stated, "the murderer thereafter fled with the 14-year old [16 years old] daughter of the murdered man," suggesting Willie Boy had kidnapped a child. These and other misrepresentations by newspapers misled the public about the tragedy suffered by the Mike family in September and October 1909.

The above-described report began a trend of writing negatively and inaccurately about Willie Boy and Carlota. Worse yet, many people with no direct knowledge of Willie Boy vilified the Chemehuevi runner. Few, if any, newspaper writers and editors knew or bothered to probe Willie Boy's character or the circumstances within the Chemehuevi community that led to the murder. One reporter claimed, "the murder was entirely unprovoked and was one of the most cold-blooded and fiendish ever perpetrated in this region." Relying on supposition, this reporter claimed Willie Boy "crept up and shot the old man with a shotgun, stepping from behind the tree as he fired the shot." The reporter maintained the undocumented commentary by declaring Willie Boy threatened "to kill any member of the family who would give the alarm." Furthermore, "Billy Boy" forced "the young Indian maid to accompany him and fled." The reported kidnapping of Carlota apparently drew more readers than a story of star-crossed lovers and an accidental shooting.

Another newspaper, the *Riverside Daily Press*, reported that "Willie Boy stole" a "Winchester repeater with 18 cartridges in it" from Arthur Gilman. Everyone writing at the time seemed to know that Willie Boy was "a dead shot," a true fact reported, at least. His skill at shooting a gun was well-known. According to local historian Maude Carrico Russell, a rancher had taught Willie Boy to shoot a rifle. Russell stated that at the age of fourteen, rancher "Frank Sabathe taught Willie Boy, how to shoot a rifle." Willie ultimately became an expert marksman and "could hit a rabbit on the run a mile away." One of the deputy sheriffs reported that "Willie Boy was an absolutely dead shot with the 30-30 rifle." The deputy "had often seen the man shooting coins flung in the air." Deputy Constable C. D. Hauverman of Banning contended that Willie Boy was "a dead shot" and could "kill a rabbit on the run a long distance away with a rifle, and I have often seen him hit coins in their air with rifle shots." As a superior marksman, Willie Boy was potentially a dangerous adversary for lawmen.

The *Riverside Daily Press* reported that Willie Boy shot Mr. Mike "in the old man's left eye and he never stirred afterwards." Hardly a reliable account, for despite the authoritative delivery the reporter was not an eyewitness. No one witnessed the shooting. The story offered pure conjecture intended to encourage a negative perception of Willie Boy and to increase newspaper sales through sensational headlines. Claims ran rampant that Willie Boy threatened to kill other members of the Mike family before he kidnapped Carlota. Maria Mike and members her family had fought with Willie Boy in the aftermath of the killing, but their interactions with reporters was little to none. In Chemehuevi tradition, speaking of the dead was avoided, and newspapermen relied largely on conjecture.

Willie Boy and Carlota fled Gilman Ranch, escaping southeast along the Morongo Hills into the Colorado Desert to the Whitewater River near present-day Palm Springs. According to William Mike's grandson, Joe Mike Benitez, his grandmother told Carlota and Willie Boy to leave, not wanting Willie Boy to hurt anyone else. Chemehuevi elders claim that Carlota loved Willie Boy. She chose to go with him, but this interpretation was apparently non-sensical to whites in the region, who asserted that Willie Boy kidnapped, raped, and beat Carlota, forcing her to go with him. Indian Agent Clara True reported the Chemehuevi runner badly abused Carlota, continually thrashing her with "abuse too horrible to describe." Without supporting evidence and possibly relying on rumors, Agent True claimed Willie Boy made Carlota carry many "burdens" including his coat, which True falsely reported Willie had stolen from a miner after murdering him. Chemehuevi claim these accusations to be untrue, pointing to the couple's earlier love and attempted elopement. The demonization of Willie Boy started immediately, depicting the man as an Indian savage and claiming he continually raped and beat Carlota on the trail. Once again, there were no witnesses to their time on the run. Reporters based their articles on the posse's stories, which claimed Willie Boy "was driving the girl before him." Preconceived notions about Native Americans helped these depictions take hold and become the accepted truth in the story of Willie Boy.

The image of the "bad Indian" – all too often conflated with "drunk Indian" – resonated with white readers of the sensational newspaper accounts. Treating Willie Boy as a stereotype rather than engage in the more complex issues leading to William Mike's death proved advantageous to the posse, press, and fiction writers who spread false rumors that Willie Boy was drunk when he killed William Mike. English colonists and American settlers had a long tradition of stereotyping Native Americans as lazy, stupid, and drunk people. The country and its news outlets often provided rumors and misinformation about Native Americans. In the case of William Mike's death, accounts of Willie Boy's drunkenness run counter to testimony that Willie Boy was not a drinker. But rumors that Willie Boy had "liquored up" to muster courage before murdering William Mike fit an all-too-common narrative about Native Americans; it also served to justify the inequities visited on Native communities by European-American settlers, both as tribes and as individuals. The lie grew with the telling: soon Willie Boy was portrayed as a dangerous drinker who posed a continued threat to Carlota and the wider community. This accusation had racialized overtones as various written sources claimed Willie Boy had to get drunk before he had the nerve to confront William Mike about Carlota.

On October 12, 1909, the *Riverside Daily Press* printed a headline announcing, "Fire Water Caused the First Murder." The writer claimed, in what would be best described as a piece of fiction, that "the young Indian was drunk when he committed the crime." The writer alleged some unnamed white boy gave Willie Boy liquor or brought it into the bunkhouse where Willie Boy was living. This reporter wrote that Willie got into the whiskey, "then in a fit of drunken rage, stole the rifle and creeping up on the sleeping Indian, fired a shot into the head, killing him instantly, and after a struggle with the rest of the Indian's family, forced the girl, whom he afterwards killed." Willie Boy had been reduced to a caricature: a cold killer acting "in a fit of drunken fury." According to historians Sandos and Burgess, *The San Bernardino Sun* and *Los Angeles Daily Times* of October 12 as well as the *Redlands Daily Review* of October 17 ran similar articles, saying Willie Boy drank two bottles of whiskey and a beer chaser before confronting William Mike. Like many other reports, posse member Ben de Crevecoeur often made false accusations many times to the press after September 26 when Willie Boy killed William Mike.

The characterization of Willie Boy as a drunk had no basis in fact. Indian Agent True and Coroner Dickinson had previously stated that Willie Boy did not drink, and no one ever reported seeing Willie Boy drunk, including his employers and ranch hands. Arthur Gilman roomed with Willie Boy, someone who'd know if alcohol was a part of Willie Boy's life; he never stated that Willie Boy drank. Demonizing Willie Boy wasn't surprising or unusual, though it interfered with finding justice for William Mike and a presumption of innocence for Willie Boy. But the public was hungry for a simple narrative that didn't challenge societal beliefs and accusing the Chemehuevi runner of being a drunk fit the bill. In another article out of San Bernardino, the reporter claimed Willie Boy was known for two things: his "brutal ferocity" and "his extreme interest in squaw beauties." Another empty and unsubstantiated claim. The reporter on this baseless article lacked knowledge of Southern Paiute communities, and he had no familiarity with Willie Boy's past experiences with women. Over time, people living within settler communities of the twentieth century accepted the stories produced by posse members, newspaper reporters, and fiction writers. They added to the legend of Willie Boy as a lady's man, kidnapper, pedophile, and rapist. In reality, Chemehuevi elders say that Willie Boy moved to the village at Twenty-Nine Palms to find a wife, settle down, and start raising a family.

Newspaper stories continually confirmed common stereotypes about Native Americans held by people living on the frontier. Some of the most prominent reporters covering the last western manhunt included James Guthrie for the *Los Angeles Herald*, Thomas Holt of the *San Bernardino Sun*, and Randolph Madison of the *Los Angeles Record*. Various newspapers spread falsehoods about Willie Boy and Carlota, including the *Riverside Morning Mission*, *Los*

Angeles Herald Express, Los Angeles Daily Times, Redlands Daily Facts, Redlands Daily Review, Seattle Star, and others. Most past writers accepted the newspaper stories as fact and uncritically perpetuated lies and half-truths. Notably missing from these written accounts is the Chemehuevi point of view. Little to nothing was understood about the *Nuwuvi* and reporters failed to consult Chemehuevi people, especially members of William Mike's family or that of Willie Boy. When one writer met with Dorothy Mike Rogers, the youngest daughter of William Mike, he didn't listen or privilege her knowledge of the family's history. He also ignored Cahuilla scholar Katherine Siva Saubel and her father, Juan.

    The impact of this cultural deafness was devastating in several ways. Had Willie Boy been brought to trial, these accounts would likely have prejudiced a jury of white men. But that's *if* he made it to trial – something the posse wanted to avoid as they satisfied the public demand for a score-settling outside of a court room. Settlers and lawmen believed American Indians were wild, vicious, and murderous, creating an aura of panic in the best of times. With the murder of William Mike and the disappearance of Carlota, the public was fine with Willie Boy being hunted down like a vile animal or rabid dog. Sheriffs of Riverside and San Bernardino Counties gave "shoot on sight" orders to their deputies, authorizing the lawmen to shoot to kill the dangerous Indian outlaw.

    On September 26, 2009, Chemehuevi elder Joe Mike Benitez opened up about his family's view of what happened. One hundred years to the day that Willie Boy killed Joe's grandfather, Joe Mike Benitez told a packed audience meeting at Gilman Ranch the following account: "My grandfather wrestled with Willie Boy. He shot and killed William. My grandmother fought with Willie Boy and told him to go and take Carlota so he would not kill anyone else." American Indians, including Chemehuevi, Cahuilla, Mojave, Quechan, Cocopa, and Southern Paiutes in Arizona, Utah, Nevada, and California endorse the Mike family's interpretation of events: Willie Boy and William Mike fought over the gun, William grabbed the barrel of the gun, and during the struggle the gun went off in his face. The bullet wound exited through the top of his head. Native Americans report that Willie Boy brought the gun because he was afraid of William Mike, well-known for his stern countenance and assertive nature. Following Carlota's wishes, Willie Boy met with William Mike in a last ditch effort to convince him that the marriage should happen. Willie Boy loved Carlota, but love wasn't enough given the close relation of the young people. When Willie Boy entered the tent of William Mike, the inevitable explosive scene ensued. As Joe Mike Benitez pointed out, the Mike family and many Native Americans believed the two men "wrestled" over the gun. Chemehuevi elder Mary Lou Brown remembered that unlike the time Willie Boy and Carlota eloped from the village of Twenty-Nine Palms, "this time the whites chased them, along with some of The People."

    School Superintendent Harwood Hall for the Malki Sub-Agency provided his own assessment of the Willie Boy affair, writing that Willie Boy "became infatuated with an Indian girl of 29 Palms who with her father was camping near Banning and who refused Willie Boy's advances. The fellow became despaerate [sic] and concluded to carry her off by force." Before allegedly kidnapping Carlota, Hall claimed that Willie Boy "shot the sleeping father" and "forced the girl to accompany him to the mountains at the point of a gun." Agent Clara True categorized Willie Boy as one of the Indian "bad boys" she managed at the Malki Agency. "The Indians here," she said of Southern California Indians, "are like bad boys." She felt the best way to manage "children" was to keep a close eye on them and "keep them busy" or else "evil" would result. True reported to Commissioner of Indian Affairs Robert Valentine she "kept them keyed up" so they would harm no one.

Agent True claimed the Willie Boy affair resulted from an Indian feud between Willie Boy's family and the Mike family, an assertion without merit. Both families had lived peacefully at the village of Twenty-Nine Palms. Friction understandably developed between the two families after the murder of William Mike, but over the course of the twentieth century, the families worked out their differences and lived peacefully with each other. The two families agreed to work together to inform historians Burgess and Sandos in the writing of their book. During one of their interviews, the historians asked the elders if they had worked out their differences, and Alberta Van Fleet remarked, "That's right, it has finally been healed now." The elders knew that the so-called Willie Boy affair resulted from tribal incest laws, which they explained clearly to the scholars. Had Agent True, Sheriff Wilson, Superintendent Hall, newspaper reporters, and modern writers bothered to consult with Native people or explore cultural values of local tribes, they might have reached a more nuanced conclusion. Knowing little or nothing about *Nuwuvi* culture, especially tribal marriage and incest laws, these narrators of the Willie Boy story delivered a skewed account.

The errors were reinforced through repetition by community leaders, including Superintendent Hall, Agent True, and Sheriff Wilson. Respected for their positions, these individuals joined forces to spin their own version of the killing of William Mike, without firsthand knowledge of what happened the night of September 26, 1909. Riverside County Sheriff Frank Wilson reported on William Mike's death, repeating the error of William's surname and calling him Boniface. In his official report written November 2, 1909, eighteen days after the posse returned home to end the great western manhunt, Wilson wrote, "Willie Boy, shot and killed Mike Boniface . . . while asleep, and seized and took away against her will from camp the fifteen year old daughter of Boniface, known as Ioleta [Carlota]." Settlers and contemporary writers referred to William's daughter by many names, including Lolita, Ioleta, Nita, and others. Her father and mother named her Carlota, and the family never changed her name. To this day the Mike family and those that know of the girl call her Carlota, and the name appears on her headstone erected by the Mike family.

There was also the allegation that Willie Boy armed himself before meeting William Mike, stealing "a .30-30 Winchester rifle from the Gilmans, and also a belt of cartridges." Willie Boy may have taken additional shells from the Gilman Ranch either before or after he shot William Mike, the *Thau Winthum* or chief of the Twenty-Nine Palms Band of Indians. There is little doubt that Willie Boy killed him around 9 pm on the night of September 26, 1909. The question centers on intent: did Willie Boy go to William Mike's tent intending to end the man's life? Or was it the equivalent of manslaughter or negligent homicide? As mentioned before, members of the Mike family and other Native Americans generally believe Willie Boy shot William Mike by accident while they struggled over possession of the rifle. No matter. Once sheriffs of Riverside and San

Bernardino Counties became involved in the manhunt, posses were formed and the search was on for Willie Boy. Riverside County Sheriff Frank Wilson reported that the day after the shooting, the lawman's office "received a telegram at 9 a.m. telling of the murder." The sheriff "immediately went by automobile to Banning." By the time Sheriff Wilson arrived in Banning to form the first posse, "Constable De Crevecoeur had found the tracks of the Indian and girl some ten miles east of Banning beyond Cabazon, leading into the mountains." In the white community, Ben de Crevecoeur had earned a local reputation as an obnoxious, untrustworthy storyteller, but he participated in the first phase of the western manhunt. Ben appears to have been the source of much of the misinformation provided to newspaper reporters who used his accounts and that of other members of the posse to provide readers sensational – and questionable – information.

On September 27, the first posse organized to hunt down and kill Willie Boy. The posse included men from the Banning area who reveled in the limelight of being part of an old-time western posse out chasing down and possibly killing an outlaw in the heart of the American West. Members of the posse initially appeared thrilled with an adventure reminiscent of dime novel plots. Exciting stories from old timers about hunting down outlaws and silent movies that glamorized westerns attracted members of the posse. Surely some of these men had seen the *Great Train Robbery*, the first American action film directed by Edwin S. Porter in 1903. The film had an all-male cast with Alfred C. Abadie, Broncho Billy Anderson, Justus D. Barnes, and Walter Cameron. Notably absent from these fictional scenarios was the idea of innocent until proven guilty or the right to a trial of one's peers. Excited posse members now had their chance, a once-in-a-lifetime-chance, to be a part of a real-life adventure to hunt down and kill Willie Boy. The posse cast themselves as heroes out to save the Indian girl, Carlota, their damsel in distress and innocent child manipulated, beaten, and sexually abused by the crazed Indian outlaw, hoping to save her life before the brutal Willie Boy did further damage. In so doing, the public would honor them and make heroes of the men riding after the Indian desperado.

The posse organized in Banning. It included Joe Toutain, Ben de Crevecoeur, Waldemar de Crevecoeur (better known as Wal), Charlie Reche, and two Indian trackers, Segundo Chino and John Hyde. One of the trackers, Segundo Chino, was forty-eight years old and was experienced as a police officer. He was a big man with broad shoulders and a keen mind. Segundo was a good shot with a handgun or rifle, and Indian and non-Indian people living in the Banning Pass knew Segundo never ran from a fight. Chino lived and worked on the Morongo Reservation in the Banning Pass where people identified him as a Serrano and Cahuilla. He was a half-brother to Pedro Chino, a famous, high level *puul* or shaman, of the Agua Caliente or Palm Springs Cahuilla tribe. Chemehuevi people claimed Segundo Chino was one of their people. He was part *Nuwuvi* or Chemehuevi.

Shortly after the posse left Banning, posse members stoked public outrage by spreading unfounded tales that Willie Boy ravaged Carlota daily. The posse concocted the "proof" of these ill deeds by claiming they could read "signs" Carlota allegedly wrote in the sand, mud, and on rocks. These claims are problematic. First, the Chemehuevi had a verbal, not written language. Second, the signs Carlota was alleged to have written have no connection to any Chemehuevi form of communication. If she wrote them – which is highly suspect – she would have no expectation that the signs would be understood. In reality, Carlota wanted to marry Willie Boy and shared in the decision to run away. It's impossible to know how Carlota felt about her lover killing the father she loved, but that doesn't mean she was unwilling to travel with Willie Boy.

After the death of William Mike, Segundo Chino joined the posse to track down his relative, Willie Boy. John Hyde, a Kumeyaay Indian, joined Segundo Chino as a tracker. Hyde's friends called him Jack, and he was about twenty-eight years old when he joined the posse – the same age as Willie Boy. At the time of his appointment as tracker, Hyde lived in the Banning Pass, but he'd grown up in the mountains of eastern San Diego County. Newspaper reporters and editors claimed Hyde was a Yaqui Indian, but Cahuilla elder, historian, and scholar Katherine Siva Saubel reported that John Hyde was a Kumeyaay or Diegueño Indian. Saubel reported that Jack Hyde came to the Morongo Reservation from the Mesa Grande Indian Reservation in San Diego County, and Hyde's name and family appear in the Registers of Vital Statistics of the Mission Indian Agency of the Indian Service. Little else is known about John Hyde, except Indians considered him a superior tracker. As a member of the posse chasing Willie Boy and Carlota, Hyde would play a critical role the upcoming manhunt.

While the posse organized in Banning, Willie Boy and Carlota traveled rapidly on foot to Whitewater. The couple had traveled by foot over the Morongo Hills, skirting the foothills of the San Bernardino Mountains. They traveled through rocky and sandy hills along an undulating trail and decided to head toward the Mojave Desert as they both knew the environment of the Mojave Desert and the landscapes they would pass through. Knowing where to find food, what to eat, and where to find springs, seeps, and *tinajas* worked to their advantage. The first destination was toward the Whitewater River, a cold, swift-flowing stream that originated in the San Bernardino Mountains, snaking its way across the Coachella Valley to the Salton Sea. Willie Boy and Carlota traveled to Whitewater River then north through the rugged and rocky terrain between the San Bernardino Mountains and the Little San Bernardino Mountains. Official reports indicated they traveled from the Colorado Desert toward the Mojave Desert by way of the Big Morongo Canyon. Willie Boy and Carlota followed an ancient Indian trail familiar to them both, which led them into Morongo Valley where they knew where to find water. The couple traveled on foot, but they both moved swiftly. With each step, they separated themselves from the posse riding on horseback. Passing through Morongo Valley, a picturesque landscape tucked under the eastern shadow of San Gorgonio Peak, they continued walking and running north, gaining elevation with every step until they reached a rugged escarpment that took them into the high desert toward The Pipes. Willie Boy and Carlota held the advantage of knowing the location of springs and *tinajas* where they quenched their thirst. At these places of precious water, they filled a goatskin bag that Willie carried over his shoulder. Along the way, Willie Boy hunted rabbits, squirrels, doves, and quail. The couple also gathered plant foods and seeds as they moved along, providing the couple nourishment.

    Upon reaching the high desert, Willie Boy and Carlota entered an area known as The Pipes, an area long used by Native Americans from many tribes. Pipes Canyon led into the eastern slope of the San Bernardino Mountains where Chemehuevi and other Indians entered the mountains. On previous trips, Carlota and her family had hunted deer and bighorn sheep in the mountains. They had gathered piñon nuts, acorns, and bear grass in the mountains with the permission of *Keeka Pakuuma*. On this trip, the couple had no time to enjoy the canyon or the mountains with the posse chasing them, but they believed they had put some distance between them and the lawmen. As a result, they rested and replenished their food supply, which proved a fatal mistake.

The area surrounding The Pipes contains pictographs and petroglyphs, painted or pecked into the rocks by ancient tribal people. While these images conveyed messages during ancient times, they don't represent a written language and certainly not 20th century Chemehuevi. Deputy Sheriff Ben de Crevecoeur made the preposterous claim that some of these images were created by Carlota, allegedly during her captivity, to provide clues for trackers to find her. According to de Crevecoeur, the signs he "read" indicated that Carlota had recently sent out distress signals to the posse. Ben and others reportedly read these signs, which told the posse that Carlota was in great distress. These ancient signs allegedly revealed that Willie Boy prodded and pushed her along the trail with his rifle, continually threatening to shoot her if she didn't keep up with his pace. Posse members reported Carlota kept stumbling, slowing her down and frustrating Willie Boy. Could Carlota have communicated through these pictographs or by drawing symbols in the mud that Willie Boy was beating her? That she wanted to be rescued by the posse? The ancient petroglyphs and rock art were created centuries earlier; any suggestion they came from Carlota is absurd and outright deceptive. As for inscribing in the earth an early 20th century version of emojis? Equally implausible. The Chemehuevi had no written language, and the markings that de Crevecoeur and others in the posse claimed came from Carlota are highly suspect as being made by her.

The men interpreted the signs and tracks as indicating Willie Boy was savagely beating the girl, stopping periodically to rape her. Ben de Crevecoeur and other members of the posse purposely promoted outright falsehoods about Willie Boy, which fit a previous pattern of misinformation. Building on prejudices and stories circulating in the hours after William Mike's death, they fed the press their own flawed interpretations. As public outrage grew, the stakes for the posse members and law enforcement became increasingly steeper. As reporters played up these untruths in numerous newspaper articles, public officials then repeated the inaccurate accounts in their official reports. Agent Clara True added to the false statements, saying Serrano *Keeka* Jim Pine had interpreted the symbols to read, "My heart is almost gone." This assertion was false. Neither Serrano nor Chemehuevi communicated in symbols of a written language, but without the balance of accurate information the public accepted this nonsense as truth. Contemporary Chemehuevi scoff at the notion that Carlota left messages in a mythical sign language. When many see the photograph of the so-called messages, they laugh out loud at the absurdity of the posse's claims.

Did Ben de Crevecoeur realize that the Chemehuevi had no written language? If he did, and it's likely he knew the truth because he'd grown up in the area and was in contact with Southern California Indians, then the charade was deliberate. The same is true of the other posse members. Ben de Crevecoeur and Charlie Reche liked the attention newspaper reporters gave them, and they vied for the top position of "knowing" more than the other. Newspapers loved lurid stories that vilified Willie Boy and made Carlota into a weak, defenseless child without agency. Settlers cast Carlota as the victim and an unwilling participant in Willie Boy's escape. So long as the great western manhunt fueled the flames of racism and Indian hating, these men could continue to insert themselves into the story and bask in the limelight.

Members of Chemehuevi and Serrano tribes knew the truth: far from being a victim, Carlota traveled willingly with the man she had once eloped with. The telltale signs are there in their escape, as Carlota actively participated in erasing their trail, and kept up with Willie Boy. The couple had grown up in the East Mojave Desert and were hearty desert dwellers. The posse and newspapers continually stereotyped Willie Boy as the wild, savage, uncivilized devil who drew on his primal instincts to steal, kill, and rape innocent Carlota, though the extreme bias is economically motivated. But the impact may have surprised even these lawmen; as the settler community dehumanized Willie Boy, that same community found it easier to kill the "animal." In fact, the public insisted the posse keep after Willie Boy until he was dead. Little distortions served to inflame the reader. For example, Carlota's age was often understated, suggesting Willie Boy was a pedophile. Newspapers and contemporary observers clamored for Willie Boy's death.

Historians Sandos and Burgess argued that non-Indians drew on old tropes to paint Willie Boy in the vilest of terms, making him a demented devil and an agent of Satan. The posse, newspaper reporters, and the public generally joined in the Indian hating, creating diametrically extreme versions of Willie Boy and Carlota that reflected competing views of Native Americans. Willie Boy was the focus of racial hatred of Native Americans generally, with all the attending negative stereotypes. Carlota, on the other hand, symbolized the good Indian, a helpless girl abused and manipulated by the bad Indian. She embodied the image of the noble savage, the foil of Willie Boy, who had become their dirty dog. Settler communities were familiar with the innocent and kind Pocahontas and Sacajawea tropes, and Carlota was framed as the Native version of a damsel in distress. It was the classic battle of civilized vs. uncivilized, wild vs. tamed, traditional Indian vs. assimilated. Stereotypes – positive and negative – had been absorbed by non-Native communities through lifetimes of family stories and popular culture. In the most extreme, the hatred focused on a violent cartoon image of non-Christian, uncivilized, barbaric, backward, and brutal Indians who they considered uncivilized and uneducable. Historians Burgess and Sandos aptly pointed out that the "Indian Hating" approach to Willie Boy was a product of the outrage shown by settlers, newspaper reporters, posse members, and authors. Settlers had an easy time focusing their hatred on one Indian. He carried the cross for all Indians in the fall of 1909, with a target on his back and a posse ready to shoot first and ask questions later.

As the posse made its way through the mountains north toward The Pipes, outrageous stories about Willie Boy and Carlota circulated throughout Southern California and beyond. Newspapers in other parts of California and across the United States ran and reran sensational stories based on hate, rumors, and innuendo. Settler subscribers to newspapers consumed the lies, because they had anticipated and expected no less about a wild Indian "buck." Writing for the Newspaper Enterprise Association, San Francisco, October 19, 1909, Randolph W. Madison – a relative to President James Madison – composed an article claiming that Willie Boy turned to murder because of "The Blood of His Fathers."

From his desk in San Bernardino, Madison diagnosed Willie Boy as having bad blood and a defective brain, which had caused him to commit various crimes and to murder William Mike. The article began with a simple statement: "He was a bad Indian" who became "a wild beast." Madison claimed that Willie Boy moved like a deranged animal. With only a thesaurus-derived store of invectives and no substantiating evidence, Madison claimed that Willie Boy's blood was so foul that he could "withstand the 'civilizing influences' of the white man (meaning largely, 'firewater' and .30-30 bullets) and to live his life, in some measure, after the pattern of his fathers and his fathers' fathers." Again, without basis in fact, Madison falsely stated that Willie Boy had kidnapped Carlota because he believed in wife capture: "If you want her, take her." Madison seems to have believed that an amorphous Indian culture allowed its men to take any Indian woman, "if she is not the squaw of another." The writer's ignorance of indigenous people is stunning, even for the time. Madison added the Chemehuevi runner had answered "the call of his blood" by murdering Mr. Mike. While pundits spread rumors and unsubstantiated stories about Willie Boy, the couple climbed rugged mountains on foot and entered an area of the Mojave Desert known as The Pipes.

Climbing out of Morongo Valley and emerging into The Pipes, Willie Boy and Carlota would have believed they were safe from the sheriff's posse. No radios or cell phones with news updates to keep them apprised of the situation, they would have assumed they were out of harm's way. At The Pipes the couple established a safe space for Carlota to rest. Willie Boy wrapped her in his handsome leather coat and handed over the water bag before setting off to hunt and gather, intending to return with food. Willie Boy left Carlota to rest in the huge boulders at The Pipes, never dreaming the posse was closing in on them. Segundo Chino and John Hyde rode in advance of the posse, following the couple's trail. Elder Mary Lou Brown provided a short, to the point Chemehuevi account of events surrounding Carlota's death. She interpreted the scene at The Pipes in this way: "Willie Boy hid his wife in a wash, gave her his coat and water skin, and went for food." Significant events unfolded while Willie Boy ran deeper into the desert to hunt and gather or break into miners' shacks in search of provisions.

    In the short time Willie Boy was gone, Carlota would be killed by a gunshot. Almost to a person, Indian people do not believe Willie Boy murdered the woman he loved. Mary Lou Brown even referred to Carlota as "his wife." Native Americans and others believe that John Hyde (or, less likely, Segundo Chino) killed Carlota by mistake. Circumstantial evidence strongly suggests that John Hyde shot Carlota while mistaking her for Willie Boy. Carlota was 5'6", two inches shorter than Willie Boy, with the same dark black hair and weighed between 120 and 130 pounds. Shorter and lighter than Willie Boy, certainly, but from a distance, she resembled him. The confusion was exacerbated by Willie Boy's "good quality, tailored" coat, a distinctive leather coat, lined with wool or fur, which Carlota was using at the time she was shot.

    The posse had moved forward following or paralleling tracks left in the sand and dirt by Willie Boy and Carlota.

Segundo Chino and John Hyde rode in advance of the posse on horseback along rocky outcroppings, marking the trail for the posse following behind. Meanwhile, Carlota was nestled in the large rocks at The Pipes. Perhaps she rested, totally unaware that the vanguard of the posse had come up on her. When she realized riders were approaching below, she began to move. From her vantage point in the rocks, she would have seen John Hyde before he spotted her. Alarmed the posse was near, Carlota began to move in the rocks. Hyde saw someone moving in the boulders, a figure similar to Willie Boy and wearing or carrying his distinctive leather coat.

Carlota's movements caught Hyde's keen eyes – his instant impression was that Willie Boy was scrabbling about in the rocks. The Deputy pulled his rifle from the saddle scabbard and prepared to fire. From a distance of 75 to 100 yards, Hyde likely dismounted and set the stock of his high-powered rifle on a rock as he took careful aim, firing off a single round. In the early morning hours, Hyde used good light to track the figure through his sights, many yards away from him. As Carlota turned to run, the crack of the rifle echoed through the rocky terrain. The bullet struck Carlota in the back and she dropped from sight behind the rocks, bleeding from the front and back of her body.

When the posse realized they had shot Carlota, they scrambled to place blame elsewhere, namely pointing the finger at Willie Boy. Newspaper reporters and government officials contributed to the spread of misinformation about Carlota's death, blaming Willie Boy and casting him as a "Double Murderer." To enhance the story of Carlota's death, several accounts claimed Willie Boy had tortured Carlota several days before murdering her. In his report to the Commissioner of Indian Affairs Robert Valentine, Indian

School Superintendent Harwood Hall stated that Willie Boy had "horribly mutilated the Indian girl and finally killed her after she became unable to go further." The newspaper *Morning Mission* of September 29, 1909 reported that the posse found Carlota's body "barefoot with feet bleeding from the cruel march" as a result of the "Indian girl . . . being forced on at the point of a gun by the crazed savage." The reporter claimed Carlota was "scantily clothed," hinting at sexual abuse.

The next day the *Morning Mission* reported, "Deputy Sheriff De Crevecoeur of Banning brought back to civilization last night the first authentic news of the hunt [about] . . . the Indian 'Willie Boy,' who is driving the girl before him across the plains." De Crevecoeur's story "reads like a tale of the old days of utter lawlessness." According to the deputy sheriff, the couple had traveled through Big Morongo Canyon and "for miles along the trail a big coyote has been following the couple keeping a certain distance from the Indian and the girl, but always picking up the trail as soon as they start on." In this uncharacteristic scenario, de Crevecoeur claimed the coyote stalked the couple like a wolf waiting for its next meal. The posse was so near the couple, de Crevecoeur said, that "they could hear her crying and talking in entreating tones to her captor. The girl appeared near to exhaustion." The lawmen faced "extreme danger in coming upon the madman without being aware of his presence." Like many elements of stories reported in newspapers of the time, Ben de Crevecoeur invented this account to gain notoriety; newspapers happily printed the unverified stories to sell newspapers.

Newspapers reported only the posse's version of the story, concurring in the narrative that Willie Boy had murdered Carlota. Reporters and other recorders of the manhunt repeated the posse's stories until the public accepted their version as factual: that Willie Boy murdered Carlota in cold blood. In the absence of evidence, a trial, or even Willie Boy's explanation of events, a false narrative promoted by posse members, with a vested interest in vilifying Willie Boy, became accepted fact. Lies and half-truths told by Ben de Crevecoeur, fellow Deputy Sheriff Charlie Reche, and others dominated the newspaper accounts. Notably, the only eyewitnesses to Carlota's death, Native Americans John Hyde and Segundo Chino, remained silent as to what had happened at The Pipes. The public embraced uncorroborated reports that Willie Boy was a wild and heinous fiend who violated and then murdered young Carlota, despite the findings of the coroner and his jury. Coroner Dickson and a Coroner's Jury found that Carlota had been shot in the back, "just behind the left shoulder." The Coroner's Report stated that the bullet entered her body and was "cutting its way downward through her breast and coming out through the right abdominal cavity." The evidence indicated Carlota had been killed by a long-distance shot, not a close shot that would have gone straight through her body.

Using evidence found in the Coroner's Report, historians Burgess and Sandos correctly stated that the bullet wound was "consistent with the trajectory of a long-range shot." They concluded, a "falling bullet hit her high in the back and exited low." If someone shot Carlota from a long distance, Willie Boy is exonerated. And if Willie Boy sought to shoot and kill his wife, he would have aimed for her heart or brain, not the back of her left shoulder. No posse member, not Hyde or Chino, ever owned up to the fact that a member of the posse shot her by accident. But news of Carlota's death caused the settler communities of the American West to further pillory Willie Boy and demand his capture or death. On October 5, 1909, San Bernardino County Sheriff John C. Ralphs issued a wanted poster, announcing, "Arrest for Double Murder." The wanted poster described Willie Boy as "slim built, walks and stands erect; yellowish complexion, sunken cheeks, high cheek bones; talks good English with a drawl; has scar under his chin where he has been shot and some teeth gone." The "Wanted Poster" further reported that on Sunday, October 3, 1909, an "Indian filling the description of Willie Boy was seen cooking a rabbit between Goffs Station and Manvel." Chemehuevi elder Philip Smith published a similar account in "Yesterdays: 50 Years Ago," saying people saw "Willie Boy cooking a jack-rabbit at Goff" in the East Mojave Desert. People from many locations in California, Arizona, and Nevada reported sightings of Willie Boy to the San Bernardino County Sheriff Ralphs.

During the fall of 1909, Willie Boy sightings occurred again and again. In September and October several newspapers reported on people announcing publicly they had seen Willie Boy in the Mojave Desert, Colorado Desert, and San Bernardino Mountains. On October 3, 1909, the *Morning Mission* reported that on the day the posse recovered Carlota's body, Willie Boy took a shot at a group of cowboys at Whitewater, several miles from The Pipes. The editor neglected to mention that Willie Boy was miles away that day, somewhere near The Pipes in the high desert, not in the low desert near Palm Springs and Whitewater. Deputy Sheriff Evans also claimed to have seen Willie Boy in a melon patch at Warren's Spring and that the Chemehuevi runner dropped his coat and ran away. These statements are ludicrous: why could Evans not catch Willie Boy when he was mounted on a horse and Willie Boy was on foot? How could Willie Boy drop his coat in the melon field, when he'd given the coat to Carlota before she was shot? Days before, the posse had returned the coat to Banning when they brought in Carlota's body. Others claimed to have found Willie Boy's tracks, reportedly "made by the hunted murderer" who had "taken refuge near Forty-Nine Palms mine." Willie Boy had reportedly "worked at this mine for the owner, Robert Swinney, a San Bernardino contractor." The *Riverside Daily Press,* claimed that Sheriff Deputy George Hewins reported finding "Tell-tale signs" that indicated to him that Willie Boy "was a very sick man," although the deputy failed to describe the "signs" or explain how he knew Willie Boy's health conditions. The *Redlands Facts* reported "a posse of 7 left Redlands for Bear Valley [in the San Bernardino Mountains] for the Rose Mine and Old Woman Springs and Pipes" where settlers purportedly recognized Willie Boy plundering cabins near the mines. Willie Boy never entered the San Bernardino Mountains during the fall of 1909.

Still another newspaper reported, it "seems to be well founded that Willie Boy has succeeded in getting a train into Nevada and has already visited the reservations." The reporter declared, "An Indian answering Willie Boy's description rode up to a ranch house in a small valley near Searchlight [on the Colorado River] and asked for provisions." Another witness maintained that "[h]e saw two men approaching up the train with rifles and did not wait for the food." Deputies reported Willie Boy was not on the Colorado River but hiding out in the vicinity of the Bullion Mountains. A Mrs. Burley reported she had seen Willie Boy on her ranchlands located a hundred miles west at Houston Flat. She felt certain she had seen Willie Boy toting a Winchester rifle.

According to Burley, the Indian she saw had a "a six-shooter dangled from his belt. Around his waist were two belts of cartridges." Burley reportedly telephoned her account to the sheriff's office, claiming she saw Willie Boy near Little Bear Valley in the San Bernardino Mountains.

Yet another account accused Willie Boy of additional murders. An Indian named "Old Jim" was discovered shot twice in the back while he was out hunting, and a newsman was certain Willie Boy had murdered him. But the report didn't stop with the death of "Old Jim," going on to claim the Chemehuevi runner had "killed two other men in the state." This account also announced that an unidentified "squaw claims that she saw Willie Boy kill a white man just after he murdered Boniface."

The alleged murder spree reached to the border of California and Arizona: one newspaper claimed Willie Boy was "also suspected of having slain a boy and a girl near Needles, also his wife and child, of whom no trace can be found." The reporter suspected Willie Boy was hiding near Searchlight on the Colorado River and planned to hide out among Southern Paiute people of Southern Nevada. Someone even claimed to have seen Willie Boy in the low desert south of the Torres Martinez Indian Reservation in present-day Imperial County near the Salton Sea. These scattershot reports were unsubstantiated, but the Willie Boy sightings helped sell newspapers while smearing Willie Boy's reputation.

Chemehuevi elder Mary Lou Brown provided one explanation of what happened to Willie Boy after Carlota's death. Brown stated, Willie Boy "came back [to The Pipes] with food but could not find his wife. He searched everywhere, but she had died." John Hyde and Segundo Chino knew the truth about Carlota's death. Given the trajectory of the shot and the fact that Willie Boy loved Carlota, it is reasonable to conclude that John Hyde, not Willie Boy, accidentally shot and killed Carlota Mike. Neither Hyde nor Chino would have hurt the girl purposely, but her death caused a conundrum for posse members who did not want to assume responsibility for Carlota's death. Realizing their problem, the posse concocted the story that Willie Boy had killed the woman he loved, implausible to contemporary Indians. Even Joe Mike Benitez did not believe that Willie Boy killed his Aunt Carlota. He stated that Sandos and Burgess had made a strong argument for Hyde killing Carlota accidentally.

Contemporary Indians believe Willie Boy loved Carlota and wanted her as his wife. They often ask why would Willie Boy kill Carlota, the person at the center of this forbidden love story? Significantly, the bullet that killed Carlota was not a direct shot. The angle of the bullet passing through Carlota entered her body near her left shoulder blade and traveled downward through her body exiting near her stomach on her right side. The trajectory of the bullet indicated a long-distance shot killed her, and the bullet killed her instantly. Her badly bruised face indicates she fell into the rocks, likely face first. After the figure moving in the rocks at The Pipes went down, John Hyde rode forward, dismounted, and climbed into the rock. He found Carlota dead, her blood pouring out in a crimson pool over the rocks and sand. Charlie Reche later claimed he found Carlota, but he was behind the Indian trackers. Hyde and Chino reached Carlota's dead body first, though Reche tried to take credit for finding the young woman.

According to the papers of writer Harry Lawton, today archived at the University of California, Riverside, Reche told Lawton that Carlota "was wearing high heels," another laughable assertion. After finding Carlota dead, the posse gathered about the body to discuss their next move. A cover story was concocted. The posse agreed to shift the blame for Carlota's death from the posse to the Native American villain: Willie Boy became the fall guy, making him the patsy for Carlota's death. The posse realized the public and the sheriffs would easily believe that the monster Willie Boy had committed this "second murder." The public easily accepted the fabrication that Willie Boy killed Carlota at The Pipes; now a double murderer in the public imagination, settlers considered him even more diabolical. The public outcry grew for the capture or killing of the ruthless outlaw.

John Hyde and Segundo Chino knew the truth of how Carlota died, but the only eyewitnesses never wrote about the event and never gave a public statement to the press, Indian agent, or sheriff. In contrast, nearly every person writing about Carlota's death at The Pipes presented their case as if *they* were eyewitnesses to her death, attesting to Willie Boy's kicking, beating, and shooting of the defenseless Carlota. Hearsay assertions rapidly became "fact" for newspaper reporters and government officials who put their own spin on accounts of Carlota's death. Riverside County Sheriff Frank Wilson wrote an official report, saying, "While on the trail the posse found the dead body of the girl. Willie Boy had shamefully abused her and killed her by shooting her in the back on the 30th [September]." In her official report, Indian Agent Clara True wrote that Willie Boy had abused Carlota so badly the agent could not provide details of the events. She said that Willie Boy's actions proved "too horrible to describe." True claimed Willie Boy forced Carlota to carry heavy burdens and his coat, writing that when the posse approached The Pipes, Carlota fell and Willie Boy "shot through the girl." True based her assumptions not on independent investigation but on the wild stories she had read in newspapers or heard from posse members, all unreliable and uncorroborated.

    Lacking substantiated and accurate reports, the public lost its ability for critical thinking, perhaps not even realizing there was a side of the story going untold. Instead, the general public accepted information provided by so-called "authoritative" sources without reservation, including the stories of sheriffs, agents, and members of the posse. For example, W. J. Hiwens, the wife of a deputy sheriff, recounted the events around Carlota's death. Hiwens announced that the "girl was shot in the back the second day of the chase." She further stated, when Willie Boy and Carlota looked "back from a rocky ridge they could see the Indian trackers and knowing that the girl could not keep up the pace, Willie Boy, standing back slightly, shot her through the back."

    Sensational stories about Willie Boy weren't just published locally. Newspapers across the United States reported the stories, perpetuating the false narrative without verifying it for accuracy. Newspapers far and wide followed the great western manhunt of Willie Boy and reported on events, including Carlota's death. One article appeared in the *Seattle Star* on October 16, 1909. "Near the spot where they found the body of little Mary Nita or Isoleta as she was known among her people, were strange hieroglyphics marked on the limestone formation with a piece of harder stone. Segundo Chino and John Hyde, two of the trackers, reportedly interpreted them as follows: 'My heart is gone. I soon will be dead.'" Carlota allegedly wrote "this message the night before she was killed by her ruthless abductor."

After finding Carlota dead, a posse member lifted Carlota's body and carried her out of the rocks. The supply wagon was used to carry her body back to Banning. Tired and worn out from their first stage of their manhunt into the rugged mountains of the Mojave Desert, the posse gave up the search for Willie Boy and returned to Banning. According to Agent True, the posse decided to return to Banning and not pursue Willie Boy so they could bring in Carlota's body for a proper burial. But it begs the question as to why all members of the posse concluded phase one of the chase rather than sending a few men back to Banning with the body and continuing the manhunt. In her official report to the commissioner of Indian affairs, True used a questionable story spun by posse members to explain their quick return to Banning town. According to the posse, "a coyote had been following them for hours and to leave the child meant that she would be eaten speedily." Many coyotes lived in the high desert, but coyotes usually ran from human contact unless they were rabid. While coyotes would eat a human corpse or that of any other animal, the posse faced no real threat from any coyotes.

The posse took Carlota's corpse back to Banning in a makeshift hearse of a horse drawn wooden wagon, moving slowly out of the mountains and high desert to the low desert near Palm Springs, crossing the Whitewater River before moving up a long grade west through the Banning Pass. From Whitewater they headed northwest, steadily climbing in elevation until they reached the town of Banning. Citizens reportedly viewed Carlota's body and mourned her death. Eventually, a deputy sheriff in Banning released her body to

Indian people who took her to the Serrano Big House located on the Morongo Indian Reservation, near present-day Chino Road not far from Ramon Road. Carlota was buried in the Moravian Cemetery on the Morongo Reservation next to her father's grave, where she lies today.

 Meanwhile, deep in the Mojave Desert, Willie Boy brought food to Carlota where he had left her at The Pipes, unaware she had been killed at the hands of the posse. At the time of Carlota's death, Willie Boy did not respond to the sound of gunfire. Apparently, he was some distance from The Pipes. When Willie Boy returned to the site where he left Carlota, she had vanished. But on the sand and rocks was Carlota's blood, evidence of her fate. The boot prints, horseshoe prints, and wagon wheels on the ground painted the picture of a posse arriving and blood being shed. Did he know that it was Carlota's blood? Or that she had died on the spot where he had last seen her? Whatever assumptions he drew, Willie Boy knew his chance of escape with his love, his wife, was gone.

 Carlota's death led the posse to temporarily suspend the chase, returning to Banning ending the first stage of their great western manhunt. It's an unexplainable tactic. Carlota was dead, they accused Willie Boy of the murder, and yet they didn't go after their suspect? Having tired of the chase, posse members returned home to rest, leaving Willie Boy on the run. As for the two trackers who were present when Carlota fell from the bullet, Segundo Chino and John Hyde said nothing publicly about the events that had transpired at The Pipes. The accidental shooting of Carlota surely sickened the two men, but if Carlota's death weighed heavily on their souls, they kept their feelings to themselves. According to contemporary tribal people, the Indian trackers drew no attention to their role in the manhunt. Other members of the posse were less discreet, reveling in the limelight and publicly spreading new tales that further enraged the public against Willie Boy. Public demands that the posse return to the Mojave Desert to arrest or kill Willie Boy became more strident, and the posse slowly reorganized. Meanwhile Willie Boy was free to hunt, gather, and steal ammunition and food from remote cabins built by miners. He used the time to locate an ambush site and prepare to engage the posse upon their return. Willie Boy believed the lawmen would surely come, and he had good reason to settle the score against them.

    The posse spent leisure time in Banning, basking in the public notoriety. The lawmen seemed reluctant to return to the Mojave Desert and the public wasn't having it. To hasten the posse's pace, newspapers fabricated new stories, claiming Willie Boy intended to assassinate President William Howard Taft during his upcoming visit to Banning, Riverside, and San Bernardino during his re-election swing through the American West. Newspaper reporters expanded on these stories, concocting yarns that Indians of Southern California, Western Arizona, and Southern Nevada planned an uprising under "Chief Willie Boy" to massacre white settlers. This wasn't the only time newspaper editors whipped up tales of an Indian Uprising intended to kill all white settlers. Nothing like stoking fear to sell papers and motivate a posse. But the claim of a pending uprising constituted a serious lie that could have resulted in Indian deaths at the hands of fearful settlers, nervous that Indians planned to assemble in large numbers and kill them. Although a hoax created by irresponsible newsmen, many people believed newspapers wouldn't lie and that Willie Boy and his followers planned a grand uprising, exhorting the posse to return to the desert and kill Willie Boy before "Chief Willie Boy" and his warriors started their own killing spree

.

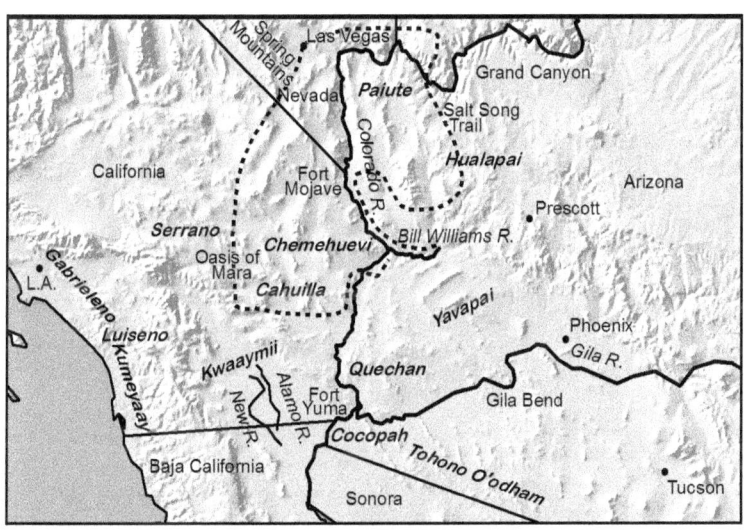

Tribal Areas and Geography of Southern California and American Southwest

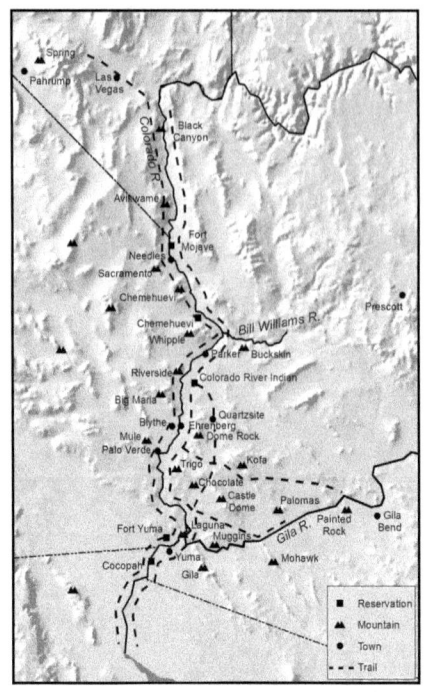

Lower Colorado River Region, Mojave and Colorado Desert

Southern California Indian Reservations

Chapter 5
Gunfight at Ruby Mountain

Rumors of an Indian uprising were a self-perpetuating myth. The more newspapers published lurid tales as fact, the more agitated white settlers became. Accounts of an all-out Indian rebellion against local communities prompted fearful responses. Accusations of an assassination of the United States president put authorities on the alert, too. Before long the press, the public, and government officials ratcheted up demands for a renewed manhunt, despite the apparent reluctance of the posse members. But the enthusiasm to capture – even kill - Willie Boy won out in the end. The posse was charged to find "Chief" Willie Boy before he carried out the planned "Great Indian War of 1909," as speculated in newspaper accounts. While focusing on the economic benefit of increased newspaper sales and advertising revenue, publishers failed to anticipate the potential violence their fantasies could invoke. The rumor of an impending Indian war could have encouraged settlers to preemptively shoot and kill Indians. Rumors had the potential of militia forces attacking Native American people or communities.

Writing for the *Los Angeles Record*, Randolph Madison spread lies about the upcoming Indian war. He reported that a settler named George Churchill from Lucerne Valley, located west of The Pipes, claimed that twenty Paiute Indians "have escaped from sv [several] reservations and are working toward Willie." He also stated "the 17 full blooded Southern Paiutes with Swaws [squaws], ammunitions and provisions [were] missing from California reservations." Like the other reports of an impending Indian uprising, neither Churchill nor Madison had any evidence that the story was true. Since

Churchill lived in Lucerne Valley, he lived miles away from any Indian reservation and did not have firsthand knowledge of an outbreak because none existed. At the same time, Churchill reported he saw Indians living in the Mojave Desert conducting "weird ceremonies and indulgin [sic] dancing and strange incantations." He may have heard of or seen Southern Paiute performing the Circle Dance or Ghost Dance Ceremonies and concocted this new story to garner interest in the upcoming Indian war. Perhaps he fabricated the story.

The *Morning Mission* offered another baseless account, claiming that Jim and Mrs. Ticup – Willie Boy's grandparents – had left an unidentified ranch in the Mojave Desert with a herd of horses that they were taking to Indian warriors, apparently to use in the upcoming Indian war. The reporter assured the reading public that lawmen were "watching them believing they will join Willie Boy in Nevada or Arizona." The newspaper article further claimed that many people traveling in the Mojave Desert had found evidence of recent fires and rabbit bones, which apparently indicated to the writer that Indians were busy preparing for war by eating rabbits. Still another report claimed Willie Boy was devouring lizards and leaving their bones to bleach in the sun, another seeming indication of war planning. As of early October, a reporter told the public that San Bernardino County Sheriff John Ralphs was out in the Mojave Desert on his own hunt for Willie Boy, apparently in a proactive measure to stop the impending Indian uprising. The reporter thought Willie Boy might be headed to Imperial County near the Arizona, and Baja California border but gave no explanation why Willie Boy had entered the territories of Cahuilla, Kumeyaay, Kamia, and Quechan Indians.

On September 28, 1909, two days after the death of William Mike and two days before the death of Carlota, the *Riverside Daily Press* ran a headline, "Outbreak Feared" and "Piutes Are On Warpath." The reporter claimed, an "Indian Uprising Imminent says Sheriff Wilson." The reporter and possibly Sheriff Wilson were convinced that "Willie Boy to Lead Natives Against the Whites." The sheriff calmed public fears by reporting, "Washington Apprised of the Grave Situation." At the time, Robert G. Valentine served President Taft as the commissioner of Indian affairs. Valentine responded in writing, saying, "no reports of trouble have been received at the bureau." However, the *Morning Mission* of October 15, 1919, reported that Sheriff Wilson had "found sure proof that the Indians are planning an uprising." Allegedly, Sheriff Wilson announced "that five Indian agents between Palm Springs and Daggett, and one near the Nevada line have filed dispatches to the Indian Commissioner Valentine at Washington, declaring in substance that an outbreak of Chemehuevis and Piutes is imminent."

The *Morning Mission* failed abysmally in this reporting. Just one Indian reservation existed between Palm Springs and Daggett, that of the Twenty-Nine Palms Band of Mission Indians, and no Indians lived there. The Indian people of Twenty-Nine Palms never took residence on the reservation platted for them in the 1890s because it lacked a water supply. Chemehuevi and Serrano instead lived nearby north of the reservation line at their traditional village next to the Oasis of Mara, the site of the famous 29 Palms Inn. That parcel of land had been purchased by the Southern Pacific Railroad without consultation or permission of Chemehuevi and Serrano Indian residents, who dwelled on the oasis nonetheless. According to the newspaper account, the sheriff learned of the Indian plan to start a war from "a [sic] agent who has been guarding the vicinity of Warren's Wells." The reporter did not identify the agent or the source of the agent's information. However, the reporter boldly stated, "The Indians received instructions five weeks ago from Willie Boy, who is regarded by his tribe as a chief, to move in small bands toward Nevada, where a tribe is to be reformed from remnants of Chemehuevis and Piutes." This was an unfounded lie.

The article in the *Morning Mission* speculated that Chief Willie Boy would "head an expedition into Nevada and establish his colony there." The newspaper reporter claimed that the unnamed Indian agent had originally received this communication "from an Indian girl near Warren's wells, two days ago." Once again, the newspaper assured the public that officials in Washington, D. C., had "been apprised of the gravity of the situation." Since the United States Army had not acted, the newspaper tried to spur some government action by reporting, "Twenty Piute Indians have escaped from Southern Nevada reservations and are working toward the Willie Boy country." In addition, "Seventeen full blooded Piutes, with squaws, ammunition and provisions are also missing from California reservations between Banning and Daggett." Basing his information allegedly on reports written by unidentified Indian agents and the sheriff – as well as the unknown Indian woman informant – the reporter stated, "Three Piute women at Old Woman's Springs remained by lighted fires all one night" where they "indulged in strange incantations and dances." The newspaper reporter intimated that the presence of three women indicated the Indians planned a war, with no basis in fact.

Under-Sheriff Wallace Evans reported he had seen the three women doing "their weird ceremonies" although he did not know the "meaning of the dance" until he discovered that Southern Paiutes from Twenty-Nine Palms and Southern Nevada "were going through the same incantations, and that on the following morning able-bodied braves were missing." Either Deputy Evans or the sheriff – or maybe the reporter – supposedly learned from "an Indian woman at Warren's Wells that this [war dance] precedes the Piutes going on the warpath, and is called the war-paint dance." The reporter further claimed that the "war-paint dance" was "part of a planned conspiracy to gather goods in preparation of war." Southern Paiute warriors reportedly initiated the opening salvo of the Great Indian War of 1909 "by killing Mr. Mike."

The reporter did not explain how killing an innocent and respected Chemehuevi elder was part of any war plan. Once again, "Indian Agent" Ben de Crevecoeur inserted himself into the story of Willie Boy. He disclosed to the reporter that Willie Boy was a chief, "descended from a celebrated Chemehuevi chieftain, known as Anger-of-the-Lightning, because of his violent temper." Ben surmised that Willie Boy had inherited his father's violent temper and may have become known as Anger-of-the-Lightning the Younger. Relying on de Crevecoeur's speculation, the reporter described a plan by which Willie Boy would dispatch his warriors against white settlers and to the precious springs in the Mojave Desert to make sure the posse did not poison the water. American Indian consultants living today on the Chemehuevi and Colorado River Indian Reservations, including members of Willie Boy's family, have never heard of anyone named Anger-of-the-Lightning. De Crevecoeur invented the character to denigrate Willie Boy and draw attention to himself.

Deputy Sheriff Evans claimed that while he searched for Willie Boy, he captured two Chemehuevi women. Evans stated the women planned to help Willie Boy in his war effort. According to one newspaper account, Deputy Evans met Mary Snyder (*So-Iris*), Willie Boy's mother, and Mrs. Ticup, Willie Boy's grandmother. Deputy Evans reported the two women were at Surprise Springs in the East Mojave Desert taking "a knap sack filled with provisions and shoes and clothing" to Willie Boy. Evans allegedly placed the women in his custody at a "ranch and held them prisoner for two days." The spring was located miles east of the Oasis of Mara, and it is questionable that the two women had traveled so far from their village during this dangerous time, but they may have been out trying to find Willie Boy. At the time, however, no one knew where Willie Boy was hiding, including his mother and grandmother. If the deputy actually captured the two women, he ultimately released them. They returned to the oasis where they later saw Willie Boy.

Southern California newspapers were actively stoking a war. Among the newspaper accounts were tales that "telegrams have been sent to all Indian agents in California and Southern Nevada." The reporter "thought that the telegrams give instructions for the calling out of troops in case of a general outbreak." The newspaper also claimed that at least twenty Southern Paiutes had "escaped from the Indian reservations in Southern Nevada and are working toward California and that portion where the Willie Boy murders have occurred." When federal troops never materialized to prevent a new Indian war, the newspaper continued to publish reports that Indians as far away as

Nevada, Utah, and Northwestern Arizona planned to join Willie Boy and attack settlers. Another account claimed that a "mysterious party of heavily armed Piutes sighted at Danby last evening are now thought to be members of this band [Willie Boy's band], which has evidently divided in an effort to throw off suspicion as to their intentions."

The Southern Paiute were accused of "seeking to protect their tribesman [Willie Boy] now sought as a double murderer." On October 16, 1909, the *Morning Mission* continued their Indian war story with the following headlines: "Outbreak of Piutes and Chimahuvis under leadership of Willie Boy;" "Government notified at Washington of Threatening Attitude of Remnants of Warlike Tribes, Who are Congregating in Large Numbers;" "Trails Lead Towards Bullion Mountain, Murderer's Hiding Place;" and finally, "Indians Have Been Hoarding Stores for Some Time – Sheriff Wilson's Posse Must Keep Moving On." In terms of the "latest from the front," the reporter claimed that Willie Boy and his own "tribe" of Southern Paiutes were "planning a war, uprising." This was total fiction. The Chemehuevi, Southern Paiute, and Southern California Indians never planned an Indian war against the settlers, and warriors never rushed to Willie Boy's aid. He survived alone with no accomplices. Alone in the heart of the Mojave Desert, Willie Boy was not part of a coordinated effort to launch an Indian war. He wasn't involved in planning an attack on settlers, and he had no plans to murder President Taft. Outside the imagination of reporters and editors eager for monetary gain, none of these allegations against Willie Boy were true. Lying turned out to be very successful, however, as the pressure generated by these stories led Sheriff Wilson to reorganize a posse and return to the high desert.

The second manhunt began in October 1909 when the posse rode out of Banning on their way to the mountainous high desert. Deputy Sheriff Charlie Reche led the posse, which included Wal de Crevecoeur, Joe Nowlin, Segundo Chino, John Hyde, and others with the supply wagon. Charlie Reche did not invite Ben de Crevecoeur, the teller of tall tales, on the second expedition to hunt Willie Boy. Unfazed, Ben continued to supply unfounded stories to reporters eager for colorful copy. Banning citizens cheered the posse as they resumed the manhunt. For the second time, the lawmen followed the same route as before, riding east through the Banning Pass into the low desert near Palm Springs. With Chino and Hyde in the lead as trackers, the posse turned north at Whitewater and rode north into the expansive desert landscape filled with colorful rocky mountains.

The posse traveled in the shadow of steep mountains of the San Bernardino range jutting into the deep blue sky, with San Gorgonio Peak rising up above all others. Additional rugged mountains sat to the east and west as well as in front of the riders. They followed the old trail that crisscrossed through the steep canyon that split the San Bernardino Mountains from the Little San Bernardino Mountains. At the top of the grade the posse rode through the Morongo Valley where they found water for their water bags and horses. Moving north the men reached another long, steep grade that took them deeper into the Mojave Desert. They reached the site of Carlota's death at The Pipes and easily found Willie Boy's trail, picking it up as it headed north and toward Ruby Mountain west of present-day Landers, California.

No one knows when Willie Boy learned of Carlota's death or who told him. But in the days following, he had stocked up on provisions, preparing, and waiting. In seeking revenge for the shooting and killing of Carlota, Willie Boy waited patiently for the lawmen. Previous writers have suggested Willie Boy moved aimlessly in circles around the Mojave Desert, but such an assertion reveals the ignorance of the writer and lack of understanding of a Chemehuevi runner. Those athletes would never waste time or energy wandering aimlessly about the desert. Willie Boy was on foot and he did not waste his time walking or running miles to the east toward the Colorado River then doubling back west to Ruby Mountain. Such accounts are absurd. In a conversation with Chemehuevi scholar Matthew Hanks Leivas and Cahuilla scholar Katherine Siva Saubel, both agreed that Willie Boy remained nearby The Pipes in anticipation of the posse's return.

    Leivas and Saubel both stated that if the Chemehuevi runner had reached the East Mojave Desert or the Colorado River, he would have remained near his people or traveled north to join other Southern Paiute in Northern Arizona or Southern Nevada. He certainly would not have traveled to the eastern Mojave Desert and then double back to Ruby Mountain located many miles west. After the posse killed Carlota, Willie Boy traveled north purposely making an obvious trail for the posse to follow. He also searched for the right place to set up an ambush, creating a blind as he had done in years past when he hunted deer, pronghorn, and bighorn sheep. Having grown up in the eastern Mojave Desert, Willie Boy learned to gather and prepare many varieties of plant foods, including yucca, dates, flowers, chia, cactus, and many varieties of seeds. Hunting, trapping, and snaring small game, including rabbits and birds, proved invaluable while holing up in the desert. Members of the posse claimed Willie Boy ransacked small shacks built by miners, and he reportedly took food and ammunition from their stores. Then he patiently waited for several days.

Willie Boy looked forward to confronting the posse, including those responsible for Carlota's wounds or death. Willie Boy believed – perhaps knew – the posse would return. They were eager to kill him, he realized, so he left a clear trail in the rocky and sandy desert for the posse to follow, especially Indian trackers, in order to establish an ambush. Willie Boy chose an ideal spot for this ambush, a place with sparse vegetation and a clear view for miles. From his vantage on the mountainside, he could see far into the distance. As the posse struggled up the steep grade into the rocky terrain to reach him, he clearly made out the dust clouds caused by approaching mounts from miles away. Ruby Mountain offered Willie Boy a remote, quiet, and open landscape where he would patiently wait for his opportunity to strike.

While Willie Boy made his way north from The Pipes, San Bernardino County Sheriff John Ralphs sent a separate posse to the Oasis of Mara to round up Chemehuevi and Serrano people and their horses, fearing the Serrano and Chemehuevi Indians living at the Oasis of Mara would aid Willie Boy in an escape. Sheriff Ralphs instructed the posse to travel to the Indian village of Twenty-Nine Palms "to scout and to prevent the relations of Willie Boy from giving subsistence and clothes to the fugitive." Agent Clara True reported that Sheriff Ralphs' smaller posse included Cahuilla leader Will Pablo, Pussyfoot Johnson, and Ben de Crevecoeur. When the posse arrived at the Oasis of Mara, posse members tried to enlist the support of Serrano leader Jim Pine. *Keeka* Pine refused to help the posse. He didn't interfere, but he also did not help them disrupt the residents of Twenty-Nine Palms.

Sheriff Ralphs sought to ensure that the Indians at Twenty-Nine Palms did not provide supplies, horses, and other forms of aid to Willie Boy, thereby helping him escape. Ralphs did not order the arrest of Indian residents, but he sent the small posse to take them and their horses into custody in Banning. Indian people then living at their village had no choice but to comply with the posse's orders to gather a few belongings and move out. Since American Indians were not recognized as citizens of the United States or of California, they had no rights under local or federal laws. Ralphs, like other lawmen across the American West, could force Indians to move at any time. Federal officials, including Agent True, failed to protect Indian rights. Sheriff Ralphs' posse forcefully removed the people and their horses from their oasis home, driving them into Banning. Once they arrived in Banning, the deputy sheriff held the Indian residents of Twenty-Nine Palms captive for a few days before releasing them. The people returned to their village at Twenty-Nine Palms. The records are unclear whether Ralphs' posse allowed the Indians to return to their homes with their horses or if the sheriff confiscated them to prevent Willie Boy from taking one or more and escaping.

Native Americans at the oasis and across the United States had no recourse when confronted with armed lawmen, militia forces, or militias. Indian men, women, children, and elders living at the oasis had the good sense not to trigger a war against the posse. Jim Pine, the senior leader of all the people of Twenty-Nine Palms, encouraged people to comply silently. The lawmen thought it possible Willie Boy would return to the oasis or other Southern Paiute villages located in the mountains of the Mojave Desert. Alternatively he might return to his former home in Chemehuevi Valley along the Colorado River, stopping at the Oasis of Mara and Chemehuevi settlements in the Old Woman Mountains along the way. The lawmen also thought Willie Boy might join one of the many Southern Paiute bands living in Southern Nevada or above the Grand Canyon. The posse kept a special eye on trails leading to the Providence Mountains and present-day Las Vegas where groups of *Nuwuvi* lived away from white settlers.

    While Willie Boy waited for the posse on Ruby Mountain, he collected a number of large rocks, which he carried by hand back to his camp high on the mountainside. After collecting rocks, he used the largest rocks as a foundation for a low but substantial rock fort or barricade from which to fight. Willie Boy designed the enclosure for one man, a breastwork from which he could fire his .30-30 at the unsuspecting posse. After laying a number of rocks for a foundation, Willie Boy placed layers of smaller rocks on top of the foundation. What emerged was a carefully constructed three-sided wall using stones and earth to buttress the dense low structure. He had no mortar, but he filled small gaps with smaller stones, dirt chunks, and debris close at hand. The structure blended with the environment.

    Willie Boy believed the posse would return to The Pipes and follow his trail northward. The trackers, John Hyde and Segundo Chino, should have been wary of the obvious trail that guided the posse to Ruby Mountain. They might have anticipated Willie Boy would prepare to ambush the posse. Knowing they would outnumber him, Willie Boy acted to improve the odds for his survival. The blind offered Willie Boy camouflage, as the rock barrier blended into the landscape. His goal was not to kill posse members as they approached the ambush, but rather relegate the posse to equal footing with him, literally, in the heart of the Mojave Desert. Once the lawmen were on foot, Willie Boy challenged the posse to see who was better prepared to survive on foot deep in the Mojave Desert.

From the slopes of Ruby Mountain, Willie Boy hid in his fortress and watched the lawmen approach. His position on Ruby Mountain gave him the advantage, much like that of Cochise's Stronghold in the Dragoon Mountains of Southeastern Arizona. Like the stronghold, Willie Boy wisely built his blind in a manner that would allow him to retreat over the rocky terrain of Ruby Mountain. Both positions provided a commanding view of the lands below and an escape route if needed. And in the case of Willie Boy, his goal appears to have been to prove who was the superior survivor: the Chemehuevi runner or the members of the posse. He knew he could outrun the posse if the posse was no longer mounted on horseback.

From Willie Boy's stronghold, he sat in calm silence, anticipating the posse's arrival. As the lawmen followed a trail leading skyward toward Willie Boy, the young man carefully moved his provisions and kit within arms' length. He waited quietly and patiently, his breastwork carefully camouflaged and blending into the mountainside. When the posse got within thirty yards or so, Willie Boy opened rapid fire, catching the posse by surprise and aiming at their horses, not the men. He killed three horses immediately and wounded another. Randolph Madison later reported that one of "the horses" Willie Boy shot "was a coal-black stallion belonging to Segunda [sic] Chino." Another horse belonged to Henry Pablo. Deputy Evans hired out one the two other horses Willie Boy shot. In addition to losing their horses, the posse lost "about $300 worth of saddles and trappings." As the shots rang out, the nervous horses panicked, jumping, jerking, and bolting. The riders had a hard time controlling their mounts. As the horses jerked about, their motion affected Willie Boy's aim and he hit Charlie Reche in the hip. The wounded deputy fell to the ground with a thud. Reche was within easy range of Willie Boy's .30-30 and an easy shot for the Chemehuevi runner, but his goal was not to kill Reche or the others. Historians Burgess and Sandos analyzed the shooting of Charlie Reche, pointing out the deputy sheriff had shiny handcuffs locked to his belt at his hip. As Willie Boy took aim, his eyes caught the dazzling reflection of the handcuffs in the sunlight that shifted his aim to the glimmering handcuffs dangling from Reche's hip. Willie Boy fired, striking the cuffs, the bullet also hit Charlie Reche.

Native American consultants believe Willie Boy killed the horses to put the posse on foot. After Willie Boy shot the horses, chaos reigned. The deputies raced for cover behind large rocks that dotted the desert landscape. Willie Boy made no effort to gun them down. When Segundo Chino angled closer to Willie Boy for a good shot, Willie Boy kept Chino at bay. The same was true when Chino tried to assist the injured Charlie Reche. Willie Boy kept Chino in check, never allowing him to get to Reche or the horses. Chino could not move without Willie Boy firing at him. From 2 p.m. until sundown, Willie Boy had every member of the posse in his sights. He controlled the situation, not the posse. Reche could not move and lay wounded in the open, face down in pain and trauma. He landed a mere thirty yards from Willie Boy. If Willie Boy had been the sociopathic killer non-Indians have made him out to be, he wouldn't have held back when confronted by a posse set to kill him or bring him in. In fact, he wasn't the calloused murderer as portrayed by newspaper reporters, posse members, the Indian agent, Sheriff Wilson, and fiction writers.

After the first round of shooting, everyone on the mountain was on foot, just as Willie Boy had planned it. Chino and Hyde quickly realized Reche needed medical help. John Hyde offered to run to the basecamp for help and bravely dashed away from the mountainside on foot. As he ran, Willie Boy shot a few warning rounds near the retreating man, but apparently didn't intend to shoot Hyde. Willie Boy was a crack shot and if he'd wanted to shoot Hyde, he could easily have hit the tracker. But he let the Kumeyaay tracker run for help. Hyde had a long way to go.

All afternoon, Willie Boy controlled the gunfight on Ruby Mountain, keeping the posse pinned down by shooting at any lawman who tried to move out of hiding. He was particularly careful about dealing with his relative, Segundo Chino, who repeatedly tried to creep forward to get a good shot at Willie Boy. The two men knew each other, and Willie Boy took no chances with Chino who was a good shot. The posse never cornered Willie Boy as newspapers later suggested. Instead, Willie Boy kept the posse pinned down for hours. Agent True reported that Willie Boy led the posse into "a regular death trap." From his elevated site, he easily picked off the horses and could have killed members of the posse. True reported that Willie Boy yelled out to the posse, "Come up here boys, I am lonely. You are not afraid of me, are you?" True was not on Ruby Mountain that day, so posse members or others who'd spoken with the posse shared this information with her in the aftermath of the gunfight.

Kumeyaay tracker Jack Hyde ran thirty-five miles in one afternoon and early evening, reaching the base camp to secure aid for Charlie Reche. Throughout the day, Hyde ran, jogged, and walked swiftly to reach the base camp, perhaps without water. In the twilight and darkness, posse members from the base camp brought up horses and a wagon and rescued Charlie Reche, who had suffered severely while lying face down in the dirt not far from Willie Boy. Reche had bled for many hours from his gunshot wound. Under the cover of darkness, the lawmen left their hiding places to tend to Charlie Reche, while the four-horse wagon climbed Ruby Mountain to rescue Reche and extract the posse. When darkness fell and the wagon arrived, the lawmen hustled Reche into the wagon bed, gathered some of their gear, and left the battlefield. Willie Boy made no attempt to stop them, perhaps slipping away in the night.

Hours before, the sun had set over the purple mountains to the west. The weather had turned cold. Members of the posse had brought coats and blankets, but they had tied these items to their saddles. Their coats were on their dead horses. In the darkness, they crawled on hands and knees to their dead animals to untie their jackets. Earlier, they had feared Willie Boy would shoot them, but the darkness provided them cover to retrieve their coats and bedrolls. Hyde and posse members from the base camp worked with the lawmen to place Reche in the wagon face down.

After the gunfight, the posse began the long journey back to Banning. In the dark desert night, they traveled slowly but steadily down to the lower desert, situating Reche to protect his injured body from too much painful jolting. The lawmen had placed Reche face down in the bed of the wooden wagon, cushioning his injuries by situating his body over a saddle padded with blankets. The trail south through the desert mountains proved bumpy and difficult. The wagon driver had to navigate over many large rocks and potholes.

The posse drove the team out of the mountains along a difficult and unimproved trail until they dropped into the low desert. From Whitewater, the trail turned northwest through the Banning Pass. When the lawmen reached the frontier town of Banning, a few posse members took Reche to the Marlborough Hospital in San Bernardino.

At the hospital, Dr. H.W. Mills cared for Reche, reporting to the press that Willie Boy's bullet had entered Reche's left hip below the hip joint, causing a jagged wound and splintering bones. After returning to Banning, Deputy Evans and other members of the posse told the press the lawmen were exhausted from the hunt and "gave up all hope of taking the man alive." Using the loss of horses as their excuse for every member of the posse retreating to Banning and giving up the manhunt for the second time, the posse nonetheless provided "remarkable" stories. Evans told reporters that members of the posse were "filled with all the hardships which accompanies such a hunt in the desert." Essentially, the manhunt and harrowing experience on Ruby Mountains exhausted the lawmen and they were not eager to continue the search for Willie Boy. Worth noting is that Evans revealed nothing about Willie Boy's condition following the gunfight and the posse's retreat. He certainly said nothing about Willie Boy committing suicide.

Reche survived the wounds he suffered during the gunfight and lived well into his eighties. But in 1909, members of the posse must have been unnerved by the ambush and gunfight, and relieved at their escape from Ruby Mountain. Watching Reche be shot and then lay suffering for hours from a serious bullet wound, they must have wondered about their own fate. Safely home, the posse knew Willie Boy was still at large with his deadly .30-30, a good reason to be apprehensive about resuming the manhunt. On the other hand, posse members may have been eager to settle the score with Willie Boy, who had shot their friend and fellow deputy, Charlie Reche, and humiliated the rest of the posse. In any case, posse members did not rush back to the high desert to restart the search for Willie Boy. Members of the posse seemed content to remain in Banning where they could rest, enjoy the early fall, and be with their friends and families. When members of the posse initially spoke to the press, they omitted any speculation about Willie Boy's fate after the gunfight on Ruby Mountain. They seemed to have lost interest in his whereabouts once they were safely stationed in Banning.

Newspaper reporters described the gunfight on Ruby Mountain in a variety of ways. On October 17, 1909, Randolph Madison provided a report appearing in the *Los Angeles Herald* that included questionable descriptions of "the most thrilling manhunt in the history of the great dreary desert." Although Madison was not part of the posse during the gunfight at Ruby Mountain, he told his readers the posse rode into a "desolate" environment where they found "the desperate Piute murderer," Willie Boy, "huddled in this lonely rock protected garrison." Two days later, the Newspaper Enterprise Association in San Francisco published another report written by Madison, composed at his desk in San Bernardino, California. Madison called Willie Boy "a bad Indian" and "a wild beast," once again stirring up racialized feelings of Indian-hating and stereotypes of the Chemehuevi runner and his people. In his article, Madison glorified the Western lawmen who had chased Willie Boy "high up among the boulders, and the cactus, and the lizards, and the gila monsters, on the slope of Granite mountain, above the desert sand, 80 miles east of this city."

Madison reported the posse had moved toward Ruby Mountain to capture or kill "Billy Boy," using a fictitious name for Willie Boy. Modern writers and an Indian artist have continued to falsify the record by using a name never ascribed to Willie Boy. The unhistorical name and unhistorical account even appears in an exhibit at Joshua Tree National Park, a disservice to the general public that knows little or nothing about Willie Boy, Chemehuevi culture, or Southern Paiute people. However, the name "Billy Boy" was germane to the historical era, as it was a nickname used at times to describe President William Taft. He was the real Billy Boy, not the Chemehuevi runner. In his newspaper article, Madison correctly reported that the Chemehuevi runner had built "a natural fortress high up on Granite Mountain," Madison's name for Ruby Mountain.

Madison argued that Willie Boy waited for the posse in his stone fort until "the posse came upon him" and Willie Boy took advantage of a surprise attack, focusing on killing horses, not the men. The ambush cost the careless posse "three [horses] dead and one wounded." This, Madison announced, "was the price the posse paid for the knowledge of the Piute's whereabouts." Apparently, one or more member of the posse told Madison that all afternoon Willie Boy "amused himself by forcing the white men to keep under cover, sending his bullets singing about their heads, cursing them, jeering at them, his laugh echoing in the crevices of the mountains." According to this account, Willie Boy had ample ammunition.

After returning to Banning, Deputy Evans reported to the press that the posse retreated from Ruby Mountain, because they lacked sufficient horses to continue the hunt for Willie Boy. Newspaper reporters and Agent Clara True asserted that the posse fled Ruby Mountain because of Charlie Reche's injury. In his official report written November 2, 1909, Sheriff Frank Wilson stated, the posse "remained on watch till nightfall" before leaving Ruby Mountain. At this point in Wilson's report, the sheriff sought to verify unsubstantiated claims made by the posse days after returning from Ruby Mountain, claiming Willie Boy had committed suicide. Initially the posse, fearing Willie Boy and his accuracy with a rifle, told Sheriff Wilson they did not stop that night to establish whether the Chemehuevi runner had committed suicide. Lawmen began to spin their account of suicide to newspapers and the public several days after the posse first returned to Banning from the gunfight on Ruby Mountain.

Chapter 6
Inglorious End

    Days before the posse set out from Banning on their third and final journey into the high desert, Deputy Wallace Evans and other members of the posse prophesized that Willie Boy was dead and decaying on the slopes of Ruby Mountain. This new assertion certainty is surprising, as no one talked about Willie Boy's death when the posse first returned to Banning from the fight on Ruby Mountains. Now they claimed to *know* this was true because as they scurried away from Willie Boy, they allegedly had heard a single gunshot. As explosive a piece of information as this was, it would have been headline news as soon as the posse reached Banning. Nevertheless, the lawmen now insisted that the Chemehuevi runner had taken his own life. Laying the foundation for finding Willie Boy's dead body on the slopes of Ruby Mountain, the posse began to feed multiple news outlets the story of "one last gunshot" several days after returning to Banning from Ruby Mountain. Caught between public pressure to bring in Willie Boy "dead or alive" and their own apprehension about coming into contact with Willie Boy again, posse members devised a plan. They'd had enough of the last western manhunt in the rugged terrain of the Mojave Desert, so they altered the story to their benefit.

    Randolph Madison composed a detailed article in the *Los Angeles Herald* on October 17, 1909. The reporter relied exclusively on testimony provided by posse members, especially Deputy Evans, but not Segundo Chino or John Hyde. If after hearing a gunshot they thought Willie Boy had committed suicide, why didn't they investigate? Posse members argued their first priority was to get the wounded Reche down the mountain and to immediate medical care for his gunshot wound. And if Willie Boy hadn't committed suicide, they wanted to get away as far as they could get from the young man's Winchester .30-30. Why did they neglect to report the shot or the possible suicide? No comment. The fact remains that Willie Boy had defeated the lawmen and prevented them taking him into custody. In a 5-to-1 faceoff, the well-armed and mounted posse members could not bring in a "deranged" lone Indian on foot. It was humiliating. Willie Boy won the gunfight and sent the posse packing, but Madison didn't write about those facts. Instead he created a ruse celebrating the gallantry of the posse. But even Madison said nothing initially about Willie Boy's possible suicide. That idea emerged the longer Deputy Evans and others rested in Banning free from the hardships of the trail.

If the newspapers of the time offer any indication of public opinion, settlers did not appreciate the posse's inactivity. Once again, the press and public wanted – eventually demanded – the posse either capture or kill Willie Boy, and they wanted to see the end result with their own eyes. Believing Willie Boy had killed Carlota, and particularly incensed that Carlota had died so young, posse members and the sheriffs were the targets of a systematic campaign, with words and headlines as the weapons. Yellow journalists especially wanted the manhunt to continue, extending the intense interest in newspaper coverage of the Willie Boy-Carlota saga. News outlets found ways to cajole the posse into a third trip into the vast Mojave Desert.

After the gunfight at Ruby Mountain, Willie Boy's movements were a source of conjecture. In official reports, white writers speculated that Willie Boy was dead. Even

Agent Clara True reported that Willie Boy was dead. Like all people claiming that Willie Boy was dead, she had no evidence to support her suppositions. People continued to speculate about what happened to the Chemehuevi outlaw. Posse members, newspaper reporters, and private citizens declared that Willie Boy was dead. Such assumptions were wishful thinking, but the unfounded rumor spread. Still, the general public demanded verification. When an Indian war was at stake, the public wanted to be sure the threat had been removed and the posse was given its marching orders: find Willie Boy and bring him back to Banning, whether in person or as a corpse. In October 1909, no one – not Indians or settlers – knew what had happened to Willie Boy after the gunfight at Ruby Mountain. Several non-Indians joined in the chorus of people announcing that Willie Boy was dead from the cowardly act of suicide, an inglorious death. The result of this third posse manhunt was predetermined, at least so far as the posse members were concerned. If the public wanted a corpse, the posse would bring one in and claim it was Willie Boy, the victim of suicide. The Indian story differed significantly, but Native Americans kept their accounts to themselves and did not share them outside of their own close circle.

    Accounts describing Willie Boy's alleged death appeared in official reports and newspaper articles before the posse left Banning. As the unfounded story of one last gunshot circulated widely it took on a veneer of authenticity and was reported as "fact" in official reports, newspapers, and family accounts within settler communities. Evans and reporters embellished the story even more both before and after the posse returned for their final journey into the Mojave Desert to find Willie Boy. The *Morning Mission* of October 10, 1909 provided a headline announcing, "Lonely Shot in Hills May Mark End of Willie Boy." Reportedly, Deputy Sheriff Evans gave the press a "Thrilling Narrative of Desperate Chase After Indian Murderer." According to the deputy sheriff, as the posse fled from Ruby Mountain, they heard "a single shot . . . in the darkness of the night following the battle between Willie Boy, the Indian murderer, and a part of Sheriff Wilson's posse."

As a result of this purported last shot, Deputy Evans excitedly told reporters that the shot in the dark signaled, conveniently for the posse, "the final chapter in the hunt for this desperate criminal." Evans reported that after the gunfight at Ruby Mountain, "his men heard the lonely shot in the hills after nightfall and were sure that the man had taken his own life." At the time of the posse's retreat, Evans asserted the mountain was "in pitch darkness." Evans believed, "Willie Boy could not have been shooting at an enemy to his freedom or at any kind of game." This story set the stage for the posse's last trip into the Mojave Desert with the predetermined account that the Chemehuevi was dead.

Deputy Evans and others, including several newspaper reporters, based their knowledge of the suicide on hearsay, speculation, and erroneous stories. The allegation of Willie Boy's suicide was just one more falsehood in a string of contrived tales involving Willie Boy, Carlota, and the exploits of the lawmen. Soon the posse, sheriff, and agent had the public believing Willie Boy was already dead, although other sources provided contradictory evidence. Apparently, the public did not receive alternative accounts very well, and newspapers noted that stories counter to the suicide narrative did not sell newspapers like the past colorful tales of the outlaw Willie Boy or war chief Willie Boy.

On October 15, 1909 a newspaper reporter countered Deputy Evans' version of his suicide story. The reporter published an account of a cowboy named Will Talmadge who was riding up the slopes of Ruby Mountain in search of grazing lands and searching for mavericks. Having read newspaper accounts about Willie Boy and the gun fight on the mountain, he rode into the area where the fight had occurred. Talmadge told the reporter, he rode horseback "close to the spot where Willie Boy battled with Sheriff Ralph's [Sheriff Wilson's] posse last week and saw no sign of the fugitive." During his ride through the battlefield, Talmadge found no human body on Ruby Mountain and he made clear that he found no sign of Willie Boy. Native Americans believe Willie Boy left Ruby Mountain after the gunfight and hid in the mountains. Later, he walked into the village at the Oasis of Mara. Contrary to assertions by Deputy Evans that Willie Boy was dead from suicide, Randolph Madison reported, "Persons we have seen in the desert are unable to give any information of the man we are after and it is presumed he is still in the Bullion [Ruby Mountain] mountain region." Some people living and working in the Mojave Desert believed Willie Boy was "fleeing toward Nevada and attempting to join the band of Piutes which it is rumored are going to his aid."

In spite of the eyewitness account by Will Talmadge, reporters and editors focused on the uncorroborated tale of Willie Boy's suicide. Deputy Sheriff Wallace Evans continued to tell reporters that he was convinced Willie Boy "took his own life" and like other officers, was "pretty sure that Willie Boy had killed himself." Evans stated that "his men are positive that Willie Boy committed suicide that night." The posse rationalized that Willie Boy only had "21 shells which were in his gun when he started out" and they estimated he had "fired 11 shots that are known by the sheriff's posse." They conveniently forgot, or perhaps never knew, Ethel Gilman's report that Willie Boy had taken approximately fifty cartridges in addition to the eighteen in the rifle. Members of the posse and the press relied on the much lower estimation and concluded that Willie Boy had used up all his shells except one, which he deployed by pressing "the muzzle of the rifle to his heart" to allow his "last cartridge" to "do its work."

Throughout the final episode of the great western manhunt, the posse continually claimed Willie Boy broke into shacks miners had built in the desert, where Willie Boy found food, blankets, clothing, and other supplies. Those shacks – at least some of them – would have housed .30-30 shells for Willie Boy's Winchester rifle. Miners, ranchers, and settlers in the American West commonly owned .30-30 caliber Winchesters, a favorite frontier rifle. Miners armed themselves while prospecting in the desert. If Willie Boy stole supplies in mining shacks, ammunition for his .30-.30 would have caught his eyes. No one really knows how many shells Willie Boy had acquired at the Gilman Ranch or in the desert mining shacks. Besides, the number of shells had no relevance to Willie Boy's alleged suicide. Yet the posse continued to promote the dramatic but questionable tale that Willie Boy had fired his last bullet by cocking his Winchester, placing his toe on the trigger, and firing the rifle into his body.

The *Morning Mission* presented the case for the manhunt to resume: "While a number of the sheriff's posse is of the opinion that the murderer has killed himself, the hunt will be carried out on the supposition that he is still alive and hidden in the mountains." On October 15, 1909, the posse left Banning town on their third expedition into the Mojave

Desert, climbing the slopes of Ruby Mountain. When the lawmen arrived at the site of the gunfight, posse members claimed they found Willie Boy dead, his body tucked under a big rock, laying in the shade. This was the same location that Will Talmadge had visited after the gunfight, finding no evidence of Willie Boy, dead or alive. The posse photographed the "corpse" they claimed was Willie Boy, placing a large black bandana or cloth over a man's face, preventing identification of the body. The photo also shows the body lying in the shadow of a large rock, and not in the rock fort from which Willie Boy had hid during his ambush.

Lawmen claimed they covered the man's face because coyotes had gnawed Willie Boy's nose and face. Out of consideration for the dead outlaw and the Indians in the posse, the lawmen masked the heavy man under the rock. In truth, the corpse looks nothing like Willie Boy, even allowing for the beginning of decomposition. Newspaper man Randolph Madison traveled with the posse on its final journey into the Mojave Desert to document the event. Given the era, he had to wait until he returned to Banning or San Bernardino to publish his reports of the inglorious end of the last western manhunt. The posse never had the satisfaction of capturing or killing the outlaw Willie Boy, but they had prophesized correctly they would find Willie Boy dead on the slopes of Ruby Mountain. Madison's account matched those of the posse members – there was no reporting on contradictory facts or convenient falsehoods.

Writing for the *Los Angeles Herald* on October 17, 1909, Madison provided a lengthy opening sentence as long winded and circuitous as the writer himself. Madison reported, "Willie Boy is dead, and with his death is ended the meteoric career of probably the most famous Indian renegade of late years, whose trail was blazed by two of the most cruel murders in the criminal annals of the two counties in which they occurred and by the most thrilling manhunt in the history of the great dreary desert, in the desolate midst of which, huddled in this lonely rock protected garrison, the desperate Piute murderer, broken in spirit by the hardships of the long chase and weak from the exposure and hunger, cheated his pursuers from their ambition of capture by using his last cartridge to end the life sought by a horde of officers whom, he thought would, in a few hours, close in on him." The posse, Madison intoned, had got their man, even if it was an unrecognizable corpse.

Madison's sensational headlines for his newspaper articles helped sell copy. For his article in the *Riverside Morning Mission* on October 17, 1909, Madison used bold type, announcing: **"Finding of Willie Boy in Heart of Desert Ends Curious TALE,"** and the **"Indian Desperado, After Terrorizing Large Area of Country Ends His own life in Jumble of Wild Rocks Near Top of Bullion Mountain."** Sheriff Frank Wilson offered a more restrained approach in his official report, written eighteen days after the posse purportedly found Willie Boy's body on Ruby Mountain. He maintained the fiction of the "one last shot" reported by the posse during their retreat from Ruby Mountain. Sheriff Wilson wrote, "When the posse had left in the evening with Reche, they heard another shot, and supposed it was intended for them, but it turned out to be the last cartridge Willie Boy had, and he had killed himself with it. The body was badly decomposed, and after full identification, it was cremated under my direction." Wilson never explained who conducted the "full identification" or how the posse accomplished its investigation. With a cremation, there would be no way to dispute the assertion that Willie Boy was dead.

Native Americans from many different tribes argue that whoever or whatever the posse cremated on Ruby Mountain, it wasn't Willie Boy because Willie Boy was not dead. Chemehuevi elder Mary Lou Brown explained the legend of Willie Boy's cremation, claiming the posse "killed an animal and burned it, or something like that." Since Willie Boy had killed some of the horses, perhaps the posse burned some of their carcasses. At the California Indian Conference in 1990, an unidentified and independent Cahuilla person gave the Indian view that Willie Boy had escaped and the cremation was a sham. His elders had told him that the family had seen Willie Boy after the fight on Ruby Mountain. During a session featuring research historians, Burgess and Sandos, the Cahuilla man "claimed that the real story was that the posse had burned an animal not Willie Boy because Willie Boy had escaped." For Indians it is a question of whether to believe accounts of the posse and reporters, who provided no substantiation, or the accounts of Willie Boy's Native contemporaries and their own family members. When it comes to veracity, especially in the Willie Boy story, there's no justification for taking the white accounts at face value. Chemehuevi and other tribes believe Willie Boy survived the gunfight on Ruby Mountain and lived out his life in Southern Nevada. The posse, they say, never captured, killed, or cremated Willie Boy, because he outsmarted the posse and escaped to live another day.

Since Sheriff Wilson didn't accompany the posse on the last trip to Ruby Mountain, his account of that third expedition has a number of holes in it. How was proper identification of the corpse carried out? When and how did he instruct his men to cremate the body? What was the basis for his "insights" into Willie Boy's frame of mind? In his report, Sheriff Wilson praised the posse for its "bravery and persistency." He imagined that after defeating the posse the night of the gunfight and forcing the lawmen to retreat, Willie Boy "was finally wore out, and used his last cartridge to end his own life." It is unclear why Willie Boy would have become fatigued and exhausted, or on what the sheriff based that assumption. Neither he nor any posse members spoke to the "double murderer." And by allegedly cremating the body, the posse erased any characteristics that could identify Willie Boy to the satisfaction of the public. Posse members told the press that they "heaped up dry brush and dead branches and there in the desert, high up among the mountains, a score of white men set flame to the strange funeral pyre of a 'bad Indian.'" Significantly, the posse did not bring in the body, take close up photographs of the body, particularly the face, and they failed to bring in Willie Boy's head to Banning to prove Willie Boy was truly dead.

On October 20, 1909, Indian Agent Clara True submitted her report to Commissioner of Indian Affairs Robert Valentine about the Willie Boy manhunt. Prior to writing the report and without reference to hard evidence, she had determined that Willie Boy had either committed suicide or the posse had killed him in the gunfight. True's assessment was short and to the point. She wrote, "Willie Boy was found to have taken his own life with his last cartridge. He took off his right shoe, placed the gun against his heart and pulled the trigger with his toe." Having no direct knowledge of what had taken place on Ruby Mountain or what the posse found or did not find on their return on October 15, Clara True relied exclusively on the words of biased individuals with their own vested interest in skewing accounts in their favor. Notably, Agent True never consulted Chemehuevi people about Willie Boy. Although Indian Agent True professed a friendly relationship with the Mike Family and Jim Pine, she never asked Indian people for their account of Willie Boy. She learned about the purported suicide in the newspapers, especially an article written by Randolph Madison the day before she wrote her own report to the commissioner of Indian affairs, and accepted Madison's version of events without questioning. She reiterated Madison's description of Willie Boy using his toe to pull the trigger of his rifle. Like the rest of the reading public, True accepted Madison's report at face value, including the details about Willie Boy's alleged suicide. This was not unique; most in the settler community seemed to accept the suicide story unconditionally, but Agent True should have held herself to a more rigorous standard.

Most important, the posse returned to Banning with no body, no head, and no conclusive photographs of the alleged dead outlaw. Native Americans familiar with the Willie Boy story, including *Nuwuvi* people from several groups and members of the Mike family, do not believe Willie Boy committed suicide. Elders often ask: Why would Willie Boy kill himself after defeating the posse and driving the lawmen away? Why would he commit suicide after successfully ambushing the posse, pinning them down all day, and driving the lawmen into a full retreat? For many Indian people, accounts of Willie Boy committing suicide are culturally nonsensical. Committing suicide was and is a serious violation of Chemehuevi cultural law, as unacceptable as incest. Those people arguing that Willie Boy committed suicide so he could join Carlota in the afterlife, are mistaken. Both infractions ran contrary to deep Chemehuevi beliefs. Contemporary

Chemehuevi elder and Salt Song Singer Matthew Hanks Leivas explained that Chemehuevi and other Southern Paiute elders "frown upon suicide," saying that suicide violates fundamental *Nuwuvi* ways of life and being, past and present.

Within *Nuwuvi* culture, man was part of creation and creative forces charged human beings to be positive and productive, not destructive. "Man was to be positive in all matters," Leivas maintained, "not negative or destructive." Suicide, Leivas continued, was forbidden because "to take one's own life is evil and against the ways of the people." Leivas disagreed with those writers suggesting that Willie Boy took his own life so he could be with Carlota in the spirit world, saying "suicide was taboo and Willie Boy's soul would be in limbo, not with Carlota." Killing himself would have kept Willie Boy's soul from entering the afterlife, which the Chemehuevi people believed was in the Milky Way. Willie Boy was aware that suicide condemned one's soul to wander the earth as a ghost, and he would not have passed through *Nuva Kiav*, the stairway to the next world. In fact, Willie Boy had to seek redemption to make his spirit right and in balance, because of the violations he had incurred by turning his back on Chemehuevi laws surrounding incest, murder, and elder abuse. If Willie Boy had wanted to kill himself, he only had to stand up behind his rock fort to allow the police to kill him. Willie Boy protected his body throughout the gun fight to preserve his life and live another day.

When the posse set out on their last journey into the Mojave Desert, Randolph Madison accompanied the lawmen to report firsthand on the killing or capture of the man Madison called, "the bad Indian" and "wild beast." Madison brought his camera along, planning to use his camera to document the "last, flickering spirit of war-fare in the western Indian" that had "flared up for a moment." Writing after October 15, Madison claimed the Indian threat posed by Willie Boy "died with him, never to disturb the pre-eminence of the white man in this domain." As the posse organized and began its last adventure, Madison took several candid photographs of the Mike family and members of the posse. Some of the photographs depict close ups of individuals, showing many details. At the gunfight site on Ruby Mountain, where the posse claimed to have found the decomposing body of Willie Boy, Madison took many shots of a body tucked under a rock in the shadow of a boulder with a black handkerchief on its face. But he failed to capture the kind of closeup photographs provided in other photographic presentations made by Western lawmen to unmask desperados and verify their kills. Law enforcement officers always sought to confirm for the public that the body seen in the photograph was, in fact, the outlaw the posse had pursued.

 Madison's photographs were full-body shots, but without close-ups of the face or identifying features of the corpse there could be no confirmation that Willie Boy's body had been found. As for the explanation that close-ups were avoided due to the sensitive nature of the subject, it is difficult to imagine that the lawmen were so sensitive to the feelings of Native Americans. The posse's similar claim that coyotes had chewed on Willie Boy's face, making it too unsettling to be photographed for public viewing holds no weight. During the nineteenth and early twentieth century, the general public participated in viewing gruesome displays of "justice." The general public often attended hangings of criminals, creating carnival atmospheres, picnics, and community sings before and during public executions.

In the annuals of the American West, many photographs exist of dead outlaws killed or executed by lawmen. Few, if any, depict an outlaw who had outsmarted the posse, won a gunfight, and chased the posse from the field of battle. The public enjoyed seeing dead bodies' graphically displayed photographs. Frontier families often took photographs of their dead relatives lying in coffins, sometimes even posing the bodies as if they were still alive with other family members. The public clamored to see detailed pictures of dead outlaws. As a result, photographers took close up and graphic photographs of John Wesley Hardin, Cole Younger, Bob and Grat Dalton, Brazen Bill, Little Dick West, Red Buck Weightman, Harvey Logan, Tulsa Jack Blake, Flat Nose Currie, and the Dalton Gang. In 1892, a posse killed Cherokee outlaw Ned Christie, known to his people as NeDe WaDe (1851-1892).

In the case of Ned Christie, lawmen had the Cook Studio of Photography of Fayetteville, Arkansas, take photographs of the dead body of Ned Christie. Lawmen had no compunction about these candid photographs of dead outlaws, often staging photo ops with a corpse and lawmen standing nearby. These candid photographs provided physical memories for posse members and proof of their kill. Lawmen hanged framed photographs of dead outlaws in their homes and offices, a badge of honor, civic duty, and proof of their kill. The photographic evidence of slain outlaws left no question in the minds of the public that the lawmen got their man or men. In addition to photographs, lawmen often set up or laid out the bodies of dead outlaws for public viewing. Lawmen reveled in displaying the bodies of their prey, much as they would a dead deer, cougar, bear, buffalo, elk, or bighorn sheep. Close up photographs of a dead Willie Boy would have provided positive proof the posse got their man and evidence that Willie Boy was no longer at large or a potential menace to society. Without a doubt the public could bear the sight of a dead outlaw's face, an Indian desperado the public had learned to hate. Madison's photographs are so undistinguished as to remain an anomaly in the history of criminal photography. For a public craving graphic proof that a "bad hombre" met his end, these alleged pictures of Willie Boy's corpse are sadly lacking.

In the past, lawmen working in the American West brought in outlaws dead or alive. Frontier sheriffs, marshals, deputies, and constables often produced the bodies of dead outlaws to show the public they had killed their man. The bodies of outlaws proved their worth as lawmen and justified the posse's expenses. They sometimes propped up and exhibited dead outlaws in caskets so people could see the dead desperado or take pictures to remember the day the lawmen had triumphed. Such was the case in Clint Eastwood's award-winning film, *Unforgiven,* when Sheriff Little Bill Daggett placed the body of outlaw Ned Logan, played by Morgan Freeman, in a casket. Little Bill displayed Ned's body in a casket set out on a wooden sidewalk next to the saloon so everyone could view Ned, the dead outlaw. This was common practice in the American West, making an example of the outlaw and threatening other criminals who might meet the same fate.

On the Western frontiers of America, at times lawmen could not bring in the body of a bad man. In those cases, such as that of Joaquin Murrieta, the officer in charge of the manhunt cut of the head of the desperado and brought it back in a gunny sack. The head was then displayed to warn others not to break the law. During the course of American history, soldiers and lawmen severed the heads of prominent Indians. Puritans cut off the head of the Massachusetts Indian leader Metacom (King Phillip); bluecoat soldiers of the United States Army cut off the head of Apache leader Mangus Coloradas; militia forces cut off the head and flayed the skin off the body of Walla Walla Chief Peopeo Moxmox (Yellow Bird); following his burial near Rock Lake in Eastern Washington, paleontologists and settlers dug up Chief Kamiakin's grave to cut off is head; in the twentieth century, a medical doctor cut off the head of Yahi Indian Ishi without protest from Ishi's so-called "friend," Dr. Alfred Kroeber of the University of California. Removing the heads of Native American leaders had occurred many times in American history, and Willie Boy's pursuers could easily have followed suit – if they had actually found the Chemehuevi runner dead on Ruby Mountain. The severed head of an Indian outlaw like Willie Boy would certainly have proven the posse had completed their task, done their duty, and got their man. Their failure to do so is telling.

While Madison's photographs were inconclusive photographic evidence, the public was assured by the posse that they had found Willie Boy dead. This particular posse wasn't particularly credible, and by October 15 had frequently repeated half-truths and outright lies to the press and the public.

Still, the posse and sheriffs reveled in their discovery of Willie Boy dead on the slopes of Ruby Mountain. Great excitement swirled through the cities and towns where settlers celebrated the death of the Chemehuevi runner. No sooner had the news of Willie Boy's demise reached Riverside, California, than a dramatic troupe pulled together a script for a play about the life and death of the infamous

Willie Boy. According to the *San Bernardino Evening Index* of October 19, 1909, "a great crowd" gathered at "the Auditorium theater on Main street of Riverside." The crowd met in the streets to see a "mellowdramer" about Willie Boy, a performance by the Hollingsworth Stock Company starring Harry Hollingsworth as Willie Boy. While the crowd waited outside the theater, someone in the street made a "blood-curdling Indian cry." This loud scream nearly caused a panic among the crowd. When the curtains finally went up, the audience received a bloodthirsty presentation. The editor of the newspaper reported, "Probably the most dramatic situation is found in the role played by Miss Austa Pierce, who is the old hag Indian witch woman." Imagine an actress portraying an elderly Indian woman as a hag and witch, publicly displaying a bias within Christian settler communities against elders, women, and the spiritual beliefs of Southern California Indians. The dramatic troupe had to make the woman a hag and malevolent witch. The Hollingsworth Stock Company, especially Harry Hollingsworth, based the presentation on the posse's story. They portrayed elder women as hags and had the posse find Willie Boy dead from suicide, the coward's path of settling his wrongs. Settlers may have believed the story, but not Native Americans.

On August 25, 2019, Chemehuevi elder Matthew Hanks Leivas stated again, and unequivocally, that his grandfather, Henry Hanks, stated that he knew for a fact that Willie Boy had escaped the posse and lived out his life in Southern Nevada. Chemehuevi chief Henry Hanks was alive in 1909 and had closely followed the last western manhunt. Henry's daughter, Gertrude Hanks, learned about Willie Boy firsthand from her father and other tribal elders, including Willie

Boy's relatives, then living on the Colorado River Indian Reservation. She passed on her knowledge to her sons and daughters, including Matthew Hanks Leivas. Henry and Gertrude Hanks explained that the posse never captured Willie Boy or found his dead body. Native Americans on many reservations in Nevada, California, Arizona and beyond, share the same view that Willie Boy survived the gunfight on Ruby Mountain. In fact, many American Indians state with certainty that Willie Boy got away, because members of their family actually saw Willie Boy after the gunfight on Ruby Mountain and in the years following 1909.

During the 1990s when historians James Sandos and Larry Burgess conducted the first substantive interviews with Chemehuevi elders about Willie Boy's fate, they heard the same refrain from every Chemehuevi consultant: Willie Boy survived the gunfight at Ruby Mountain and lived out his life in Southern Nevada. When historians Sandos and Burgess asked Chemehuevi elders what happened to Willie Boy after the gunfight at Ruby Mountain, every elder replied that the posse never killed Willie Boy and he did not commit suicide. Mary Lou Brown told the historians, "He didn't die from the posse. How could they catch him? He ran like the wind." Brown concluded that after the gunfight at Ruby Mountain, Willie Boy "ran further, far out into the desert, away from his family." *Nuwuvi* people "later heard that he had died" of tuberculosis.

Alberta Van Fleet, a descendent of Willie Boy, adamantly announced, "The posse never got him." Willie Boy, she said, "got away to Nevada" and he died years later of tuberculosis." Joe Mike Benitez, the senior member of the Mike family, echoed reports that Willie Boy survived the gunfight at Ruby Mountain. In an email to the author, Joe added that Willie Boy eventually traveled to the village of Twenty-Nine Palms to see his mother and grandmother. According to Joe, when Willie Boy left the village at the oasis, he sequestered himself in the mountains north of the Oasis of Mara. Joe learned these facts from his mother, Susie Mike, daughter of William Mike. She told her son that Willie Boy eventually worked his way north through the Mojave Desert and villages located along the Bullion Mountains and north past Tecopa and Shoshone to the small Southern Paiute village called Pahrump. The Mike family reported that Willie Boy left the oasis heading north before continuing in that direction of southern Nevada. Joe Benitez felt that Ben de Crevecoeur "spiced up the story by telling they had shot [the foot off] and cremated his [Willie Boy's] body in the desert." First, Joe explained, "I don't think the family [of] Willie Boy would have allowed it and I think they would have come to claim the body." Joe agreed with Burgess and Sandos that a member of the posse shot Carlota by mistake, because Willie Boy "left her his jacket to keep warm." Joe reported that when fiction writer Harry Lawton contacted his mother, Susie Mike, "my mother would not talk to him. So who did Lawton talk to?"

    On September 26, 2009, one hundred years to the day when Willie Boy killed William Mike and the last great western manhunt began, Joe Mike Benitez became the first member of the Mike family to provide his family's assessment of what happened to Willie Boy. He spoke at a symposium sponsored by the Riverside Historical Society held at the Gilman Ranch Museum in Banning. Approximately 150 people assembled at the ranch to hear Joe Mike Benitez, Larry Burgess, Zoe Erickson, and Clifford Trafzer. During the lecture by Benitez, the grandson of William Mike, Joe elaborated on the oral history his mother had shared with him. Based on the author's notes of the lecture, Joe explained, "none of my uncles spoke of Willie Boy. That was tradition. We do not speak of the dead. It is a bad thing to do." Joe announced to those in attendance that this was the first time a member of the Mike family had spoken publicly about Willie Boy. In fact, this was the first and only time in Joe's life that he spoke publicly about his grandfather, grandmother, Aunt Carlota, and Willie Boy. He first told the audience, "it is eerie to be here. This is where my grandfather was killed. I was not here. My mother was four years old when it happened, but she told me she remembered." Susie Mike remembered the trauma suffered by the Mike family and residents of Twenty-Nine Palms when Willie Boy killed Susie's father and ran away with her big sister, Carlota.

Joe Mike Benítez continued his lecture, saying, "I reserve the right to withhold some information," but "my grandfather was a shaman, a good medicine man. There are good and bad medicine men." Joe remembered his mother saying that William Mike "sang the songs" to bring his familiar to him and heal others. "In 1909, they had an incident" when "a person named Willie Boy" tried to marry Aunt Carlota." When Willie Boy asked William Mike if he could marry Carlota, "William Mike told him not to pursue it." When Willie Boy entered William's tent the night of September 26, 1909, Willie Boy shot and killed William Mike before he and Carlota disappeared into the desert night. After Maria reported the murder to the sheriff, Joe's grandmother "took the family back to Twenty-Nine Palms."

According to Joe Mike Benitez, "Willie Boy was on foot when the posse chased them." Joe knew that "Willie Boy was a magical runner. Spirits took care of him." When the "posse went after them," the posse "could not catch Willie Boy" because of his swift running. At The Pipes, Willie Boy went for "supplies and ammunition then back to The Pipes but could not find her." Willie Boy, Joe argued, "figured the posse had taken Carlota." Joe declared, "My mother said Willie Boy was never caught by the posse. Willie Boy went to Las Vegas and lived there." Other members of the Mike family have also stated that they believed that the posse never captured or killed Willie Boy. Cahuilla elder Katherine Siva Saubel told the author in conversation that her Grandpa, Segundo Chino, told her father and her that Willie Boy escaped from Ruby Mountain and lived out his life in Southern Nevada.

In her book, *A Dried Coyote's Tail*, Saubel stated, "they never caught him" and all the people here [in Arizona, Nevada, and California] know that the boy ran back home again." She reported that Segundo Chino had told her the posse threatened the Indians working with the posse, saying, "Don't tell anyone that he got away from us." For many years, Indian trackers said nothing, fearing the lawmen might hurt their families. Saubel speculated that the posse never found Willie Boy dead and no human body was cremated. Rather, she maintained, "They caught something, maybe a coyote. And they burned it." Cahuilla elder Chona Dominquez also claimed, "The police pursued him, but they never got near him." Like so many Indian people who know the story, tribal elders in the year 2020 believed Willie Boy got away and lived among Southern Paiutes in Nevada. The posse claimed Willie Boy was dead because in so doing, the lawmen could stop hunting him. But the story also unwittingly opened a pathway for the Chemehuevi runner to leave the area and quietly move to Southern Nevada, since the posse claimed he was dead. The lawmen no longer pursued Willie Boy and the Chemehuevi outlaw no longer feared the posse pursued him. However, Willie Boy had to face a much more significant reckoning as he dealt with the wrongs he had committed against his culture, family, and *Nuwuvi* people. He was responsible for bringing violence and death to others. According to tribal elders, Willie Boy traveled to Pahrump to face his Creator, ask for healing, and speak to his sacred mountain.

Chapter 7
Redemption and Retrospective

After the gunfight at Ruby Mountain, Willie Boy hid out in the Bullion Mountains of the Mojave Desert where he knew the location of water supplies and Native foods. Unaware that the posse claimed he had committed suicide, Willie Boy hid in the mountains away from cattlemen and miners until he felt sufficiently safe to move closer to the village at Twenty-Nine Palms. Willie Boy likely watched for a short time to make sure the posse had not stationed deputies in the village to capture him if he returned to his old home. After the killing of William Mike, Maria and the Mike family returned to their home at the oasis. Willie Boy's grandmother, mother, and aunts had remained in the oasis village when others had left weeks earlier to work at the Gilman Ranch.

During the hunt for Willie Boy, Sheriff Ralphs' deputy sheriffs had temporarily but forcefully removed the Chemehuevi and Serrano residents of Twenty-Nine Palms, because Ralphs feared the people would aid in Willie Boy's escape and participate in the Indian uprising prophesied by local newspapers. Neither Sheriff Ralphs nor Sheriff Wilson understood that the residents of Twenty-Nine Palms carried a great deal of resentment for Willie Boy. Far from defending him, they called him out for violating the tribal incest law and for the deaths of William and Carlota Mike. Willie Boy had not pulled the trigger that killed his beloved Carlota, but it was his actions that led to her untimely death. People at Twenty-Nine Palms bore a grudge against Willie Boy and were angered by his selfish actions.

The Riverside County coroner and sheriff turned over the bodies of William and Carlota to William's widow and

Carlota's mother, Maria Mike. Days had passed and the family held their traditional *Yagapi* or Cry Ceremony on the Morongo Indian Reservation. The Mike family did not have time to take the remains of their loved ones back to Twenty-Nine Palms for Cry Ceremonies. Instead, they held their sacred ceremony on the Morongo Indian Reservation. With the help of Jim and Matilda Pine as well as Serrano people living on the Morongo Reservation, the Mike family held the *Yagapi* at the Serrano *Kishamnawhet* or Big House. The people would have sung Salt Songs during the wake for Mr. Mike and Carlota. Traditionally, a lead singer, usually a Chemehuevi shaman, led a group of male singers in the ancient song complex that sang the soul into the Milky Way and brought the living back into life on earth through the Salt Song Trail. At the Serrano Big House located near the Moravian cemetery, men and women sang death songs that took the souls on the Salt Song Trail to *Nuva Kiav* and into the Milky Way.

The family buried William Mike and Carlota Mike next to each other in the Moravian Cemetery on the Morongo Reservation. Not far from their graves, the Mike family buried numerous others in the quiet, windswept cemetery that faces Mount San Jacinto and sits on a slope overlooking the Banning Pass in the shadow of Mount San Gorgonio. During the years following Mr. Mike's death, various Mike family members buried their loved ones in the same cemetery to be close to William, Maria, and Carlota. In September and October 1909, residents of Twenty-Nine Palms returned to their village at the oasis. They tried to reestablish their former lives but found life difficult with the loss of their leader, William Mike, who had died in such a brutal manner. The people worried that perhaps William Mike's spirit had been disturbed by the violent and tragic way he died, and that his spirit might be at unrest within the village. According to Joe Mike Benitez, most residents of Twenty-Nine Palms chose to leave their desert homes and move to Indio where they were to live on the Cabazon Reservation. For many years, government agents had wanted the people to move into the Coachella Valley, but had never forced them to leave the oasis paradise.

After the gunfight on Ruby Mountain and the short incarceration of the desert oasis dwellers, Indian residents of the Twenty-Nine Palms returned home. Billy and Nellie Mike returned to the oasis with the other Chemehuevi and Serrano people. Nellie's parents used the surname of Holms and had moved to Twenty-Nine Palms during the late nineteenth century. Nellie married Billy Mike, one of the sons of Jim Mike, the first *Thau Winthum* or chief of the Chemehuevi tribe of Twenty-Nine Palms. Billy Mike was one of many nephews of William Mike and had a close relationship with his cousins, the children of William Mike. At the time, the children of William and Jim Mike considered each other brothers and sisters. Billy and Nellie Mike lived at the oasis village on the present-day site of the 29 Palms Inn. They were at the village when Willie Boy returned home in October or November 1909. None of the Indians living at the oasis village that fall kept a written record of Willie Boy's visit to Twenty-Nine Palms, but years later Nellie Mike provided oral testimony about Willie Boy's last visit to the Oasis of Mara.

In the 1940s, Nellie Mike Morongo visited the graves of her family and friends buried at the Indian cemetery on Adobe Road in the modern town of Twentynine Palms. While visiting the grounds of the 29 Palms Inn, she met local historian Maude Carrico Russell. Naturally curious, Russell asked Nellie to provide an interview, and the Chemehuevi elder agreed to share her historical account. By this time in her life, Nellie had lost her first husband, Billy Mike, to a gun accident. The family buried him in the Moravian Cemetery on the Morongo Indian Reservation near the graves of William and Carlota Mike. In the aftermath of this family tragedy, Nellie married Tom Morongo, a Serrano Indian and member of a leadership family on the Morongo Indian Reservation where the couple resided. Still, Nellie Mike Morongo kept in close touch with her family and friends among the Twenty-Nine Palms Band of Chemehuevi.

When Nellie met Maude Russell, she agreed to provide an oral history to be used in a newspaper column Russell wrote entitled, "Yesterdays at Twentynine Palms." Russell's oral history with Nellie also appeared in a book length manuscript preserved at the Twentynine Palms Historical Society located in the Old Schoolhouse adjacent to the 29 Palms Inn. Russell interviewed Nellie Mike Morongo about a number of topics, including Willie Boy and the volatile day he visited the Indian village of Twenty-Nine Palms. According to Nellie, she was at the oasis village after the gunfight at Ruby Mountain and saw Willie Boy when he passed through on his way to Southern Nevada. Willie Boy boldly walked into the village carrying his .30-30 Winchester rifle and wearing a leather gun belt with cartridges. He'd been hiding in the mountains west of Twenty-Nine Palms before arriving to visit with his grandmother and aunts. It is not clear if his mother, Mary Snyder, still resided at the oasis village or if she had returned to the Chemehuevi Valley or to the Colorado River Indian Reservation. Nellie Morongo told Russell that when Willie Boy entered the village, he went first to his grandmother's home on the north side of the palm trees not far from the garden. Once there, he unburdened himself by taking off his leather gun belt and leaned his rifle against an adobe wall of his grandmother's home.

At the time, Mrs. Ticup was home. According to Nellie, no sooner had Willie Boy set aside his gun and gun belt then Mrs. Ticup accosted her grandson. Most likely his aunt or aunts joined the grandmother. Together, the elderly women of Willie Boy's family harangued him for disobeying tribal laws, for killing Mr. Mike, and for causing Carlota's death. Apparently, the runner's presence drew a crowd around the home of Mrs. Ticup, as everyone was curious to see the scene unfold and hear the exchange between the elder and her grandson. Mrs. Ticup assailed Willie Boy for his deliberate, disobedient, and evil actions. In the Chemehuevi Indian world view, Willie Boy had put all of the people at Twenty-Nine Palms at jeopardy for sickness and chaos by his lawless acts, which defied tribal and state laws. His insistence on taking Carlota as his wife – despite their close affinity - led to Carlota's death.

Mrs. Ticup accused her grandson of turning his back on his cultural ways, continuing to scold him until he couldn't take the tongue lashing any longer. He walked away from his grandmother. As Willie Boy began to leave the grounds surrounding his grandmother's home, Mrs. Ticup grabbed Willie Boy's .30-30 rifle and gun belt, tossing them into a nearby irrigation pond located today on the grounds of the 29 Palms Inn. According to Maude Russell, Nellie Mike Morongo "told me that soon after the slaying of Mike and his little daughter Mrs. Waterman [Ticup] was the one who got Willie Boy's gun and ammunition and threw them into the irrigation pond in order to keep Willie Boy from continuing his rampage." Willie Boy reacted angrily, grabbing his grandmother and violently shaking her for destroying his weapon and ammunition. In his rage against his grandmother, he hurt her badly. Then, without his weapons and ammunition, Willie Boy left the village, running pell-mell into the desert north of the village and into the mountains.

When Nellie last saw Willie Boy, he was running swiftly toward the Bullion Mountains north of the village of Twenty-Nine Palms. Willie Boy ran deeper into the Mojave Desert, forever leaving his family and friends. "Mrs. Nelly Morongo said that for that act Willie Boy 'beat her up' terribly, which beating-up was probably the cause of her death, for she was a very aged woman." Days after Willie Boy fled the oasis in a rage, villagers found Mrs. Ticup dead. They carried her body into the ceremonial house, prepared her body, and held an all-night *Yagapi* ceremony. The Chemehuevi and Serrano community of Twenty-Nine Palms sang her on the Salt Song Trail to *Nuva Kiav*. After the all night sing, Mrs. Ticup's family and friends buried her on the south side of Jim Mike's grave. Her body now rests in the Indian cemetery on Adobe Road adjacent to the 29 Palms Inn.

In 2009, the author asked Joe Mike Benitez what his mother, Susie Mike and daughter of William and Maria Mike, had told him about Willie Boy. Joe confirmed that Willie Boy had come into the village at Twenty-Nine Palms after the gunfight on Ruby Mountain to see his grandmother and aunts. Benitez provided no information about Willie Boy's rifle and ammunition, but Joe said he had learned from his mother that Willie Boy left the village after his violent encounter with Mrs. Ticup. When the author asked Joe, "did your mother say where Willie Boy went after leaving the village at Twenty-Nine Palms?" On June 5, 2001, Joe Mike Benitez wrote the author saying, "Cliff, my mother always said Willie Boy had gone north and hid out in a cave until things cooled down and then went to live with relatives in Piute country." Other Chemehuevi tribal elders say that Willie Boy ran across the desert north of the Oasis of Mara, living for a time in the Bullion Mountains.

After living in the Bullion Mountains, Willie Boy began his journey north across the Mojave Desert to *Pah-Rimpi* (Water Rock), commonly called Pahrump in Southern Nevada. A group of *Tudinu* or Desert Indians lived at Pahrump. Like Willie Boy, they were *Nuwuvi*, and they shared the same tribal codes with Chemehuevi people. Through the "moccasin telegraph," they learned about the killing of William Mike, the death of Carlota, and the gunfight at Ruby Mountain. They did not know that Willie Boy intended to relocate to the village of Pahrump. From the Bullion Mountains, Willie Boy traveled north toward the present-day town of Baker, California, passing the edge of the Devil's Playground and the contemporary Mojave National Preserve. Passing the Cronese Mountains southwest of Baker, Willie Boy traveled to the frontier town of Tecopa, California, named after *Nuwuvi* Chief Tecopa. Willie Boy knew he would find water in Salt Springs, Willow Springs, or the Amargosa River before he continued on to Shoshone Springs near the present-day entrance of Death Valley National Park. Along the way, Willie Boy passed Nopah Peak to the east and the Shadow Mountains to the west, following an ancient *Nuwuvi* trail through the Shadow Mountains now known as Highway 178. As he approached the Southern Paiute village of Pahrump, Willie Boy saw his sacred mountain, *Nivagaanti*, (Charleston Peak) in the Spring Mountains to the east.

On October 6, 2012, the author camped in the tall trees of the Spring Mountains on the slopes of Snow Mountain with his friend and colleague, Matthew Hanks Leivas. A number of *Nuwuvi* men, women, and children had camped in the heart of their creation mountain to enjoy some family and cultural time together. The people reconnected with other Southern Paiute people and families as well as their sacred mountain. The weekend included a trip through the Sheep Mountains to the Las Vegas Mountains where a number of people collected piñon nuts before returning to the camp site on Snow Mountain. During the pinion gathering, the author asked Matthew Hanks Leivas and an accomplished indigenous scholar who wished to be anonymous if they would discuss Willie Boy. They both agreed. After an evening meal, the small group met in a picnic area where a number of *Nuwuvi* people had built a large fire and had begun to sing traditional songs. The evening turned darker and the air became chilly. The author and two Southern Paiute scholars sat on a picnic table, the author taking notes of this impromptu and friendly discussion.

Nuwuvi people living on reservations in California, Arizona, and Nevada stated unequivocally that after Willie Boy left the Oasis of Mara, he walked to the *Nuwuvi* village at Pahrump, Nevada, located about sixty miles west of Las Vegas, Nevada. The young scholar indicated that Willie Boy had no relatives at Pahrump. When asked why Willie Boy had traveled to Pahrump, the *Nuwuvi* scholar replied, "he came to Pahrump because of our hill!" Then he explained in great detail about the spiritual power of the surrounding area of Pahrump Valley, including a sacred hill. *Nuwuvi* people of Pahrump served as the gate keepers of their sacred mountain within the Spring Mountains. A great deal of spiritual power existed and remains today around Pahrump. The region is tied to "many forms of water," including numerous springs and artesian wells where spirits lived in the waters. The people consider Devil's Hole a very powerful place, a site where souls traveled to the underground.

    The entire region near Pahrump had a direct and profound relationship with the Southern Paiute sacred creation mountains that include *Nivagaanti* or Mount Charleston, the holiest of mountain peaks. Southern Paiute people far and wide considered Pahrump, Ash Meadows, and the Pahrump Valley infused with healing power. The region contained many "doctoring spots on the west side of the mountain" and Willie Boy traveled to Pahrump "to get healed." Willie Boy had violated the Southern Paiute song of creation. In going against the song, the cultural ways of the people, he had ignored the cultural norms governing the people. "Marriage laws are very significant" and elders had taught *Nuwuvi* people "not even to think about having a relationship with a close relative." To do so was unfathomable, so Willie Boy's transgression of incest laws affected the entire Southern Paiute world in a negative way. "It was not the murder as much as the other things" Willie Boy had done that threw him and the *Nuwuvi* world out of balance. In the belief system of Southern Paiute people, Willie Boy's wrongs radiated out to every *Nuwuvi* person at the time and for all time, because the culture of the people connected everyone in a covenant. Cultural sickness in one area of Southern Paiute Country affected all the people.

    Chemehuevi elder Mary Lou Brown provided her view of Willie Boy and Carlota's bad actions when she told historians Burgess and Sandos that Willie and Carlota "did what was wrong. Sometimes young people are like that; they want what they want. But they were too close, first cousins, I think, and it could not be permitted. The girl wanted it as much as he did." Alberta Van Fleet, a member of Willie Boy's family, agreed with Brown, pronouncing that the couple were first cousins and should not have been married. Among *Nuwuvi* people, couples had to be nearly six generations apart in order to marry. Both Carlota and Willie Boy shared in breaking cultural incest laws, which continues to weigh heavily on *Nuwuvi* people today. The Southern Paiute scholars added that breaking marriage rules "was a huge violation" that cost Carlota and Willie Boy their families, lands, and resources. *Nuwuvi* people would "ostracize the violators" and their evil actions could cause sickness, starvation, and drought.

Once Willie Boy "threw life out of balance... he needed power to neutralize" the wrongs he had committed. The list of offenses was short but intensely serious, the latest of which attached to his own grandmother. Willie Boy broke a cultural norm against abusing one's elders when he violently shook this elderly woman, which led to her broken heart and death. Willie Boy had truly walked away from Chemehuevi culture and the ancient spiritual teachings of *Nuwuvi* people. To find some peace and begin his journey to find balance in his life, he traveled to Pahrump. In the holy Pahrump Valley in the shadow of his holy mountain, Willie Boy sought Indian spiritual medicine to help him become right again and in tune with his culture. Willie Boy journeyed to Pahrump in search of balance and redemption.

When Willie Boy arrived at the village of Pahrump, the people congregated in their ceremonial lodge where men and women talked about what they should do about the Chemehuevi runner. Willie Boy posed a threat to the villagers, because lawmen might charge villagers with aiding and abetting a known criminal. At first members of the Pahrump community decided to banish Willie Boy from their village, agreeing on that plan until the village shamans entered the meeting. The shamans had questioned Willie Boy about his purpose in coming to Pahrump. They shared what they had learned with the people attending the community meeting. The shamans explained that Willie Boy had come to Pahrump for spiritual healing and described why he needed to remain at their village. When Willie Boy arrived in the village he visited a holy hill connected spiritually with *Nivagaanti,* the holy mountain. According to elder and singer Larry Eddy, Red Ant Hill was part of the Salt Song Trail and the hill had a direct and potent spiritual connection with *Nivagaanti* – Mount Charleston. Power flowed throughout the Pahrump Valley and in the vast space between Red Ant Hill and Mount Charleston. That ancient power still exists, as Southern Paiute people well know. During an interview between the author and Chemehuevi elder Larry Eddy on March 5, 2016, Eddy identified the hill. "We sing about that mountain near Pahrump. It is an early morning song. It is the 'Mountain with Big Ants' or Red Ant Hill near Pahrump. We sing that song in Mojave language. It has connections with the underworld." In the song cycle of Salt Songs, singers travel south of Pahrump to "sing a song about Night Hawk when the songs reach Joshua Tree at the Oasis of Twenty-Nine Palms." Today, the 29 Palms Inn is located on sacred ground, the former home of many Chemehuevi and Serrano people. The Inn is located on property that housed two powerful and holy ceremonial lodges, and owners of the Inn protect the area where the lodges once stood, never permitting desecration of the sacred sites found or construction on the property. The relatives of Chemehuevi and Serrano people are buried along the tree line and in the cemetery off Adobe Road. The 29 Palm Inn is situated on lands related to the Night Hawk Song that Salt Song Singers still reference during their all-night ceremonies of beautiful sadness.

When Willie Boy arrived at Red Ant Hill, he could see *Nivagaanti* in the distance to the east. From Red Ant Hill he "talked to the mountain." Larry Eddy explained that Southern Paiute people "speak" to the mountain. "I speak to the mountain. We speak to that mountain, Mount Charleston. We start in the evening songs and speak to the mountain. We return to Charleston Peak when we die." Eddy continued, saying "Mount Charleston has a Spirit. That is the place where there are steppingstones to take us through the hole in the sky." Willie Boy traveled to Pahrump for redemption, to be healed for all the ways he had violated important cultural conventions. He had lost his way, his song. So he walked to Red Ant Hill to begin a new journey, one that would take him back into his culture and restore a semblance of balance. The shamans from Pahrump learned of Willie Boy's wishes when the leaders asked the young man why he had come to Pahrump. When the shaman learned Willie Boy "wanted to start to make things right, to set things in balance," the shaman "called the wind" and asked for the healing to begin.

Snow Mountain "is a body" and the shaman "used various parts of the body" to doctor people. They called on parts of their sacred mountain to begin a slow process of helping Willie Boy put his world back together again. After hearing what the elder *puahgaants* had to say, the villagers of Pahrump agreed that Willie Boy could live among them during his spiritual healing. Since Pahrump was "a gateway to power," Willie Boy remained in the village to live out his days. Spiritually, he worked toward putting his life in balance by admitting his transgressions and following tribal laws.

Southern Paiute people from Pahrump, Parker, Las Vegas, Havasu Landing, Indio, and Coachella told the author that Willie Boy had visited their people, traveling and working among them. In so doing, several families have stories about their interactions with Willie Boy after the gunfight at Ruby Mountain. Willie Boy had walked a "hero's journey" that led him through a personal hell of his own making, but toward the end of his life, he returned to *Nuwuvi* beliefs to bring his body and soul in balance.

While living at Pahrump, Willie Boy became spiritually reconnected with his roots, his *Nuwuvi* upbringing, and the lessons elders had taught to him in his youth. He found solace in accounts of tribal creation and the healing the power of *Nivagaanti*. Remembering what he'd learned about Silver Fox and the significance of Salt Songs as a means of healing brought comfort and recovery. He learned to appreciate and use the many waters found in Pahrump Valley where spirit people resided and offered themselves to the people, especially in underground water places. During the time Willie Boy lived at Pahrump, he coped with an internal demon that ate at his lungs. He sought support and healing from all the best medicine men in the region. In spite of his reconnection with *Nuwuvi* spirits, Willie Boy contracted tuberculosis through his interaction with settlers or Indians carrying the disease. Some said his tuberculosis resulted from his past refusal to abide by traditional marriage laws or for the killing of William Mike. Shaman helped him cope with his staying sickness or spirit sickness, but they could not cure the tuberculosis that ate at his lungs. Shaman tried to doctor one of their own, "but all the best doctors could not save him from the respiratory disease."

Some elders say Willie Boy sought help at a sanatorium or place of rest for tubercular patients, perhaps at Laughlin, Nevada, though no one really knows Willie Boy's ultimate fate. Two tribal members at Las Vegas Paiute believed he died at Pahrump where the people quietly laid him to rest in that holy ground in the shadow of Snow Mountain. They sang to *Nuva Kiav* on the Salt Song Trail, the path to the Milky Way. Native Americans say Willie Boy ended his life with his people, returning to his cultural ways and finding his Chemehuevi song once more. Upon asking his mountain and Creator for redemption, he received it. In 2009, exactly one hundred years to the day after the death of William Mike, his grandson spoke for his mother, saying "my mother said Willie Boy was never caught by the posse." Willie Boy lived long enough to seek redemption and speak truth to his mountain, completing his personal quest to rejoin the body of *Nuwuvi* people.

Chapter 8
Chemehuevi Diaspora and Survival

At the close of the Willie Boy affair, residents of Twenty-Nine Palms had a rough time adjusting to life. The violent deaths of William, Carlota, and Mrs. Ticup destabilized the community, creating a cultural and spiritual unbalance at the Oasis of Mara. For several years Malki sub-agents within the Mission Indian Agency tried to move the Indians living at Twenty-Nine Palms into the Coachella Valley or Banning Pass. But those living at the Oasis of Mara enjoyed their isolation, away from settlers and with their sovereignty intact. However, in the aftermath of the Willie Boy affair, the people at the oasis met in the Serrano Big House to discuss their future and opted to relocate to the Coachella Valley. According to Joe Mike Benitez, the Indian Service did not force the people of Twenty-Nine Palms to move away from the oasis, but the people feared spiritual disturbance by William Mike's ghost if they remained at Twenty-Nine Palms. It was their choice to leave their desert home and move into the Coachella Valley. In life, William Mike had been a powerful *puahgaant*, a healer and medicine man. The people believed his spirit had the ability to create disturbances among the desert dwellers. Perhaps spiritual disturbance had already begun by the time the people met and decided to leave Twenty-Nine Palms.

Jim Pine and his Serrano followers decided to move to the Mission Creek Reservation, located southwest of Twenty-Nine Palms in the foothills of the San Bernardino Mountains due north of Whitewater. Agent Clara True offered Chemehuevi land at the Morongo Reservation in Banning or the Agua Caliente Reservation in Palm Springs, but the people refused to go there. Instead, they chose to move due south of Twenty-Nine Palms to the Cabazon Indian Reservation near Indio, California. For many years, Chemehuevi had lived in or near the towns of Indio and Coachella, working on ranches. Some of the people had married members of the Torres Martinez Indian Reservation south of Indio and some intermarried with other Cahuilla Indians. This was familiar territory for the Chemehuevi of Twenty-Nine Palms. In 1910, the Indian Service added 640 acres to the Cabazon Reservation to be held jointly by the Twenty-Nine Palms Band and the Cabazon Band of Cahuilla Indians. After the arrangement had been made between the Chemehuevi of Twenty-Nine Palms and the Indian Office, the people planned to move south to the Cabazon Reservation.

Joe Benitez pointed out that Chemehuevi had long traveled a well-worn trail from the Oasis of Mara over the Little San Bernardino Mountains south to the Cabazon Reservation in Indio, California. Today, the trail falls within the boundaries of Joshua Tree National Park. Some of the people took that trail over the mountains to reach their new home, while others traveled on the wagon road from Twenty-Nine Palms to Whitewater and from there southeast to Palm Springs and further east to Indio. No military escort forced the people to Cabazon Reservation, as the people willingly removed themselves to Indio. Lily Mike, the oldest son of William, and Jeff Boniface, one of the sons of Jim Mike, led the people into the Coachella Valley. Perhaps unsurprisingly, the Indian Service made these arrangements without consultation with the Cahuilla residents of the Cabazon Reservation. Nevertheless, the Office of Indian Affairs enrolled the Chemehuevi from Twenty-Nine Palms as members of the Cabazon Tribe. The agency had not prepared the Cahuilla to receive their new "members." When the Chemehuevi arrived, the Cahuilla gave the Twenty-Nine Palms Band a cold reception. Soon members of the Twenty-Nine Palms Band of Mission Indians dispersed in different directions, some going to live on the Torres Martinez, Agua Caliente, and Morongo Indian Reservations. Initially, none of the Chemehuevi remained on the Cabazon Reservation. But in the 1940s, Susie Mike, daughter of William and Maria Mike, returned to the Cabazon Reservation and requested an allotment of 40 acres. The leadership of the Cabazon Reservation agreed to allot her this acreage from the remaining lands added to the reservation in 1910 when the Chemehuevi families arrived. In the 1940s, Susie Mike and her son, Joe Mike Benitez, became residents of the Cabazon Reservation, which has been Joe's home since childhood.

Lily Mike moved his family to Palm Springs where he worked as a carpenter for residents there. His daughter, Jessie Mike and her children, lived with Lily Mike and the children grew up in Palm Springs. In the 1970s, Jessie's sons, Dean and Darrell, as well as her daughter, June, helped reorganize the Twenty-Nine Palms Band of Mission Indians. For many years Dean served as tribal chair before his nephew, Darrell Mike, took over the leadership role. Dorothy Mike Rogers, the youngest daughter of William and Maria Mike, also lived in Palm Springs, and served as the tribe's leader after the family lost Lily Mike. During the Chemehuevi diaspora of 1910, Nellie and Billy Mike moved onto the Morongo Reservation. Billy worked as a cowboy on various ranches in the Banning Pass until Billy's tragic shotgun accident. When Billy died, Nellie married Tom Morongo and lived out her days on the Morongo Reservation. Jeff Boniface lived in the east Coachella Valley where he lost his first wife. He then married a woman from the Soboba Indian Reservation and moved there to live with his wife's people. William's wife, Maria, married the Indian tracker Segundo Chino, and lived out her days on the Morongo Indian Reservation. On September 17, 1932, Maria died of bronchitis and pneumonia and was buried on the reservation. Her headstone identifies her as Maria Mike, not Maria Chino. Many of the people associated with Willie Boy and the Mike family are buried at the Moravian Cemetery off Chino Road on the Morongo Indian Reservation. The Mike family has their own family area where they buried their people during the years following the tragedy of 1909. Although a diaspora of the Mike family occurred after the Willie Boy affair, the families remained in contact with each other throughout the twentieth century and reorganized as a sovereign tribe during the 1970s. Members of the Twenty-Nine Palms Tribe remain united today and continue to contribute to the well-being of their neighbors in the Coachella Valley, Twentynine Palms, and the reservations located along the Colorado River. Periodically, tribal members return to Havasu Landing, near the location of their ancient village in Chemehuevi Valley.

From 1910 to the 1970s, Mike family members and other Chemehuevi families in the Coachella Valley continued their familial relationship with each other. The Bureau of Indian Affairs recognized them as tribal members of the Cabazon Band of Mission Indians until the 1970s, when leaders of the Cabazon Tribe approached the Mike family with a proposition. Cahuilla Indians of the Cabazon Reservation proposed to separate the two tribes and offered the Twenty-Nine Palms Band a portion of the Cabazon Reservation. In 1910, the government had added 640 acres to the Cabazon Reservation to be held jointly by Cahuilla and Chemehuevi people. By the 1970s, Cabazon had allotted all of the land to their tribal members—including Susie and Joe. Cabazon leaders asked the Chemehuevi if they would like to accept approximately 200 acres of unallotted land and create their own tribe, federally recognized by the Bureau of Indian Affairs. In this way, the Twenty-Nine Palms Band could become a separate Native nation with a land base of 200 acres in the Coachella Valley. According to Dean Mike, the Chemehuevi began meeting informally at the homes of various people, especially Dorothy Mike Rogers. The families met as a tribal group and discussed this offer, which the council decided to accept. Members of the Twenty-Nine Palms Band of Chemehuevi had never lived on the Cabazon Indian Reservation, and they had not been active members of the Cabazon Band of Mission Indians. Through an act of the House of Representatives and the Senate of the United States, a bill passed to split the Cabazon Indian Reservation and create a new Twenty-Nine Palms Indian Reservation. The bill also provided federal recognition for the Twenty-Nine Palms Band of Mission Indians. In 1975, President Gerald Ford signed the legislation into law, thereby recognizing the independence of the Twenty-Nine Palms Band of Mission Indians.

While many political and legislative actions unfolded nationally and in California during the 1960s, Chemehuevi families living in the Coachella Valley and on the Colorado River learned that Hollywood planned to make a movie about the Willie Boy affair. The movie was based on a book released in 1960 by Harry Lawton titled, *Tell Them Willie Boy Is Here*. A movie by the same name starring Robert Redford, Katherine Ross, and Robert Blake began production. In 1969, the film featured a cast that included Cahuilla Indians, but the film did not involve Chemehuevi people, an insensitive oversight since the Willie Boy affair principally involved Chemehuevi Indians, not members of other Indian tribes. Principals making the film never consulted descendants of William Mike or Willie Boy. At the time the film was made, several Chemehuevi lived in the Coachella Valley and along the Colorado River, but the film's producers ignored Chemehuevi families whose relatives had been directly involved in the sordid affair of 1909.

Tell Them Willie Boy Is Here follows themes set down by Lawton in his book, portraying Willie Boy as a drunken, abusive, and self-centered double murderer. The movie presented negative and unfounded themes based on newspaper accounts published in September and October 1909. For many years after the great western manhunt, special newspaper issues and popular magazines continued to portray Willie Boy as a drunken rapist. Unsubstantiated and erroneous accounts of Willie Boy even appeared recently in an exhibit fabricated at a Joshua Tree National Park, thereby promoting false information about historical events and characters. The film continued the misrepresentation on an international level, but altered themes found in newspapers and other publications by providing an exciting ending to the movie. Rather than portray Willie Boy committing suicide, the movie ends with the heroic Deputy Christopher Cooper, played by Robert Redford, working his way into position for a genuine western gunfight with Willie Boy. In the final scenes of the movie, "Coop" stands face to face with Willie Boy for a dramatic shootout. After beating Willie Boy in the gunfight and killing the Chemehuevi runner, Coop learns that Willie Boy's Winchester has no ammunition. Coop realizes he had been party to a police suicide. So ends a movie primarily wedded to the posse's interpretation of events.

Chemehuevi people have generally felt the 1969 film misrepresented their historical and cultural past. Even the Native speakers in the film did not speak *Nuwu*, with Indian actors speaking their own indigenous language rather than the language of Chemehuevi people. Many elements of the film proved disappointing for those familiar with the historical account. The film was not a documentary, targeting a large audience with no familiarity with the Chemehuevi or the Willie Boy story. The old film failed to represent Chemehuevi culture, to acknowledge the Mike family or the Chemehuevi story. *Nuwuvi* people from the Twenty-Nine Palms Band, Chemehuevi Indian Reservation, and Colorado River Indian Reservation as well as many other *Nuwuvi* people felt Hollywood and the principals involved in the making of the first Willie Boy film had betrayed and poorly represented Chemehuevi people. When Sandos and Burgess interviewed Chemehuevi elders on the Colorado River Indian Reservation, Adrian Fisher remarked that when he took Alberta's mother and aunt to the drive-in theater to see, *Tell Them Willie Boy Is Here,* the women remarked, "That's not right, nobody did that, that's wrong. What are they talking? That's not Chemehuevi and it sure isn't Paiute or Mojave. What is it?" Some Native American actors in the film spoke Cahuilla, not Chemehuevi, so the elders were upset over the film's lack of representation of their culture, language, and people.

In the Spring of 2019, actor Jason Momoa contacted Chemehuevi Indian leadership and Robert Redford about his plan to produce and direct a new full-length motion picture about Willie Boy. While visiting the Mojave Desert,

Momoa had learned bits and pieces of the Willie Boy story, so he reached out to Chemehuevi tribal people about a new telling of the Willie Boy story, and the possibility of their involvement in the new film. Being indigenous himself, Momoa displayed an innate sensitivity about portraying Native Americans accurately, as reflected in his consultation of *Nuwuvi* people. Momoa was determined that this telling of the Willie Boy story would accurately portray Chemehuevi culture, language, song, and story.

Chairman Darrell Mike has served the Twenty-Nine Palms Tribe for many years. He and his family supported the creation of *The Last Manhunt*. Four of the Mike children had parts in the movie. Courtesy of the Twenty-Nine Palms Tribe.

Dean and Theresa Mike have contributed greatly to the growth and development of the Twenty-Nine Palms Tribe and the historical revitalization of the Chemehuevi people. Author's Photograph.

Chemehuevi leaders and Mike family members, Joe Mike Benitez, Dean Mike, and Darrell Mike. They are shown here during a blessing ceremony on the Twenty-Nine Palms Indian Reservation in Coachella, California. Author's Photograph.

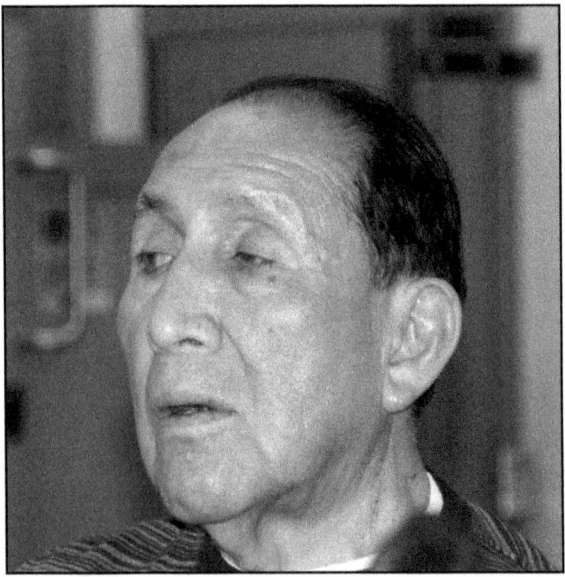

Serrano elder, educator, and singer Ernest Siva helped lead the blessing ceremony in September 2019 at the Gilman Ranch in preparation of filming *The Last Manhunt*. Author's Photograph.

Spiritual singer Kim Marcus contributed to the blessing ceremony before the start of *The Last Manhunt*. Kim led a number of Southern California Indians and the audience in a traditional blessing, blowing smoke to accompany a collective prayer. Author's Photograph.

Dr. Daisy Ocampo, Assistant Professor of History at California State University, San Bernardino, attended the blessing ceremony to begin the filming of *The Last Manhunt* in a good way. Jason Momoa graciously took his picture with Daisy and many other participants. Courtesy of Daisy Ocampo with permission of Jason Momoa.

At the beginning of *Nuwuvi* time, Wolf and Coyote created the Salt Songs to establish a song trail that led to the hole in the sky and entrance into the Milky Way. Salt Song singers sang their sacred songs at the Old Woman Mountain Preserve, just as singers did during the funerals of William and Carlota Mike in 1909. Courtesy Cultural Conservancy.

Vivienne Jake, a *Nuwuvi* woman from the Kiabab Paiute Tribe of Northern Arizona sang Salt Songs at the Oasis of Mara and Old Woman Mountains. With other Southern Paiute people, Jake initiated the Salt Song Project that has encouraged young singers to continue the ancient song complex. Courtesy of the Cultural Conservancy.

Roland Maldanado and Matthew Hanks Leivas sang Salt Songs at the 29 Palms Inn, singing to the sacred environment surrounding the Oasis of Mara. Children also danced the *Nikapi*, or Circle Dance of Southern Paiute people on the grounds of the Inn, the former site of the Indian village at Mara. Author's Photograph.

Joe Mike Benitez offered blessings of a Chemehuevi headdress worn only by *puahgaants* or shaman during ceremonies. William Mike wore a feathered headdress during ceremonies. Author's Photograph.

One evening during the filming of *The Last Manhunt*, this group of Chemehuevi men and women sang Salt Songs and later danced the *Nikapi* or Circle Dance that will appear in the full length motion picture. Matthew Hanks Leivas stands in the middle of the group holding a staff of power. Author's Photograph with permission of the Chemehuevi singers.

John Smith and several other singers joined the cast of *The Last Manhunt* to sing Salt Songs and one Ghost Dance song. John's son and daughter also sang to bring authenticity of the movie. Author's Photograph with the permission of John Smith.

For many years, Robert Chavez has given his time to support the larger *Nuwuvi* community as a Salt Song Singer. Robert lives on the Chemehuevi Indian Reservation at Havasu Landing, California, but travels widely to sing for other *Nuwuvi* communities. Author's Photograph with the permission of Robert Chavez.

Salt Song singer Joseph Drum prepared for the Ghost Dance sequence at Gilman Ranch. The singers danced the *Nikapi* at nightfall. Joseph and other singers drew on their individual and collective sovereignty, deciding to share an authentic Chemehuevi Ghost Dance song for movie viewers. Author's Photograph with the permission of Josheph Drum.

This is a facial shot, showing white clay smeared on Joseph Drum's face in preparation of the Ghost Dance sequence of *The Last Manhunt*. Nuwuvi people used the term *Nikapi* to describe the Circle Dance, a derivative of the Ghost Dance. The people still dance the *Nikapi*. Author's Photograph with permission of Joseph Drum.

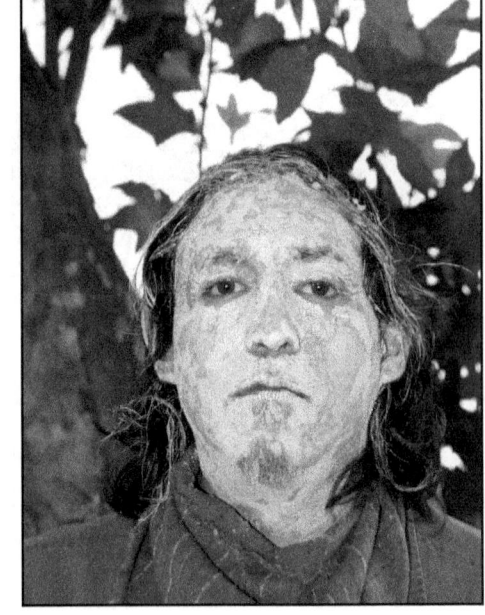

After the wardrobe artists dressed Abby Eddy Fernandez for the Chemehuevi song sequence, she posed briefly for this photograph at the Gilman Ranch in Banning. Abby was one of the few elders who participated in the Salt Song and Ghost Dance sequences of the movie. Author's Photograph with permission of Abby Fernandez.

Abby Fernandez, Matthew Leivas, and Iris Burns Leivas take a break after singers practiced their songs and awaited conducting a Ghost Dance that evening at the Gilman Ranch. Author's Photograph with permission of Abby, Matt, and Iris.

Zahn McClaron is a well-known and seasoned Lakota actor. He played the important role of William Mike, the tribal elder Willie Boy shot to death in 1909, which ignited the great western manhunt. Author's Photograph with permission of Zahn McClaron.

Lily Gladstone, a Blackfeet and Nez Perce woman, is an accomplished actress who played the role of Maria Mike, wife of William and mother of young Carlota. Lily posed for this photograph in Palm Canyon on the Agua Caliente Indian Reservation. Author's Photograph with the permission of Lily Gladstone.

The talented young actress Mainei Kinimaka is seen here between scenes on the set in Palm Canyon near Palm Springs, California. She played the starring role of Carlota, the daughter of William and Maria Mike accidently shot to death by the posse. Mainei and her sister, Maluia, are world-class surfers working in the movie industry. They both contributed significantly to the success of the *The Last Manhunt*.
Author's Photograph with permission of Mainei Kinimaka.

Martin Sensmeier relaxed in the shade under the trees in Palm Canyon on the Agua Caliente Indian Reservation. Martin played the starring role of Willie Boy, the young Chemehuevi runner who murdered William Mike and destabilized the Indian Community at the Oasis of Mara, the Mike family, and his own extended family. Author's Photograph with the permission of Martin Sensmeier.

One of the many locations used for *The Last Manhunt* included Palm Canyon on the Agua Caliente Tribe's parks. The tribe generously gave Momoa permission to shoot parts of the movie in their tribal park. The Washingtonian Palms seen in this photograph are native to California and grow naturally in the canyon. Author's Photograph.

The set depicting the Chemehuevi and Serrano village of Twenty-Nine Palms included rounded homes, including this one built by Native Americans as a movie set. This is one of several forms of houses built by American Indians of Southern California. Author's Photograph.

This is a larger version of a Chemehuevi house built by Native Americans to depict the Indian village at the Oasis of Mara. All of the material culture shown in the film was authentic and added to the reality of the built environment seen in the film. Author's Photograph.

In addition to rounded lodges, Chemehuevi and Serrano also built rectangular homes like the one in this photograph. Notice the grain basket on top of the house or on stilts next to the house to prevent rodents from robbing the family of mesquite beans and acorns. In the background in the shade is an A-framed home.
Author's Photograph.

Chapter 9
Jason Momoa's *The Last Manhunt*

From the start, Momoa consulted with the leadership of the Twenty-Nine Palms Band of Mission Indians. Darrell and Dean Mike, direct descendants of William Mike, discussed the film with Momoa and with the tribal council of the Twenty-Nine Palms Band of Mission Indians. For the Mike family, Willie Boy was not a hero but the cause of familial and tribal trauma that still exists. Out of respect for the Mike Family, Momoa kept the descendants of William Mike apprised of progress during the planning stages of the film, *The Last Manhunt*. He also contacted Chemehuevi living on the Colorado River, seeking their insights during the planning stages of the film. When Jason Momoa's Pride of Gypsies Production Company became involved in development and production, several representatives sought the advice and involvement of Chemehuevi Indians.

The production company's affirmative and proactive actions to engage Native Americans associated with the Willie Boy story was laudable and unprecedented. Momoa served as both an actor and Executive Producer. He assembled a talented group of skillful people to help drive the film, including Director Christian Camargo, Screenwriter Thomas Sibbett, and several experienced producers. Momoa also looked to Chemehuevi elder and Salt Song Singer Matthew Hanks Leivas and the author for historical and cultural information. Leivas provided authentic information on language, songs, settings, themes, and presentation. Momoa and his screenwriter, Thomas Sibbett, assured Mike family members that the Pride of Gypsies would portray the Willie Boy story as accurately as possible. At the same time, they wanted to give audiences relatable human themes through a colorful historical drama.

In an effort to be inclusive of Native Americans and specifically Chemehuevi people – including members of the Mike family – Jason Momoa, Christian Camargo, and the producers within the Pride of Gypsies conducted a conference call with the leadership of the Twenty-Nine Palms Tribe to ask its consent for the film project to go forward. In a dramatic and heartfelt telephone call, tribal leadership agreed the film should be made. Clearly, the tribal leadership trusted Momoa and his crew to represent a new interpretation of the events surrounding the Willie Boy affair. On that basis, Momoa and other production leaders moved forward under the expert direction of Christian Camargo. Before filming began at Gilman Ranch – the location where Willie Boy killed William Mike in 1909 - leadership within the production company insisted that the film begin in an indigenous way, with an un-filmed, traditional blessing offered by regional tribal members.

From the beginning, all principals associated with the making of *The Last Manhunt* worked for an honesty in presenting historical events and the people involved in the Willie Boy affair. This foundational commitment began with Jason Momoa and became the guiding principle of everyone involved with The Pride of Gypsies Production Company. Momoa originally planned to direct and play a major role in *The Last Manhunt*, but as the months of 2019 unfolded, his commitment to other projects made it impossible. Momoa turned to a friend and colleague, Christian Camargo, an experienced and highly acclaimed actor and director, to direct the project with the help of several experienced and committed producers, including Eric Laciste, Dan Clifton,

Brian Andrew Mendoza, Michele Cicero, and Martin Kistler. Deeply committed to the story, Camargo agreed to direct the movie despite the short timetable for him to begin.

Learning about Willie Boy, Carlota, William Mike, Maria Mike, and Chemehuevi people in general, Camargo threw himself into the detailed work involved in creating a motion picture. A new team organized for *The Last Manhunt*, and principals spent hours reading print literature about Willie Boy, visiting Chemehuevi people, and traveling to places germane to the story. Actual locations associated with the Willie Boy affair, including such sites as The Pipes, Twentynine Palms, Ruby Mountain, became familiar sites. The production crews and some of the actors traveled to reservations to meet Chemehuevi people and learn more about *Nuwuvi* culture. Tribal elders, singers, historians, and leaders offered historical details that could be woven into a moving story that audiences will grasp on a human level.

Throughout the spring and summer of 2019, Director Camargo and producers Laciste, Cicero, Kistler, and others continued consultations with Indian people and examined possible sites for shooting the movie. Working with his new team, Camargo pulled together thousands of pieces. Meanwhile, Charlotte Royer and her team including Willie Pink, Tony Soares, Sugie Fisher, and Manny focused on creating the built environment of a Chemehuevi village during the period. Royer paid special attention to historical photographs depicting the Indian village at the Oasis of Mara as well as other Chemehuevi villages seen in *Native Americans of Riverside County, A Chemehuevi Song, The Hunt for Willie Boy,* and other books featuring historical photographs of Chemehuevi housing and material culture. Royer employed her talents to present authentic Indian houses of the period using natural materials found at Twenty-Nine Palms thereby elevating the visual presentation of the film. In addition, she provided representative material culture, especially baskets and pottery associated with *Nuwuvi* people. Her work enhanced visual elements of the movie as did the costuming.

Camille Brenda added to the authenticity of the movie by providing wardrobing that matched the clothing of men, women, and children during the era among Chemehuevi people. Camille and her assistants provided Indian singers and dancers period dress, including aprons and scarfs for all the girls and women. Brenda spent hours researching books and special collections for historical photographs of Native American dress of people living in the Mojave Desert and Colorado River during the early twentieth century. Photographs found in the Harry Lawton Collection in the Special Collections Division of the Rivera Library at the University of California, Riverside, proved especially useful. Makeup for the singers and actors was discrete and professional, especially the white clay applied to the faces and hands of singers during the Ghost Dance scene. The dancers appeared truly ghostly on screen during a dramatic and authentic depiction of the spiritual ceremony. William Mike vehemently opposed the Ghost Dance Movement and embraced traditional religious beliefs and power found in the ancient *Nuwuvi* religion. However, Willie Boy had participated in the Ghost Dance, a practice that did not endear him to William Mike. Before agreeing to share in a Ghost Dance song and dance, Leivas asked the Chemehuevi singers if they thought it appropriate to share authentic songs. The singers agreed it was time to sing the songs and dance, offering a part of their culture to a world-wide audience.

    Momoa, Sibbett, and Camargo decided to weave into the film the tension resulting from Willie Boy's participation in the Ghost Dance, but before beginning shooting, they wanted the Native American participants in the film and local Cahuilla and Serrano Indians to offer a blessing. Matt Leivas gathered a number of Indian singers to offer a traditional Native American blessing, praying for success and safety of participants in the film. Such a blessing was characteristic for a movie played by several indigenous people and those sensitive to the spiritual ways of American Indians. Jason Momoa, Christian Camargo, Thomas Sibbett, the producers, and others eagerly supported a Native American blessing to kick off the filming. As a result, on the night on September 26, 2019 – ten days short of 110 years after the fateful murder of William Mike – Chemehuevi Salt Song leader Matthew Hanks Leivas officiated a traditional American Indian blessing that kicked off the filming of *The Last Manhunt*.

    Singers from Southern California and the Great Basin reservations gathered at the Gilman Ranch in Banning to offer their prayers, songs, and music. Through song and prayer, they collectively asked the Creator to watch over the filming and ensure no harm came to the people involved in the movie. Singers prayed for authenticity in the depiction of the human drama and tragedy involved in the Willie Boy affair. Chemehuevi elder and singer Matthew Hanks Leivas served as the Master of Ceremonies for the gathering. The evening began with the masterful music of Henry Vasquez providing an hour of soft music from an Indian flute. After an hour of flute music, Cahuilla leader Kim Marcus, Serrano elder Ernest Siva, and a group of Native American men offered a Tobacco Ceremony, blowing smoke in the four directions of the earth thereby sending their prayers to heaven in the smoke drifting skyward. When the ceremonial leaders turned in the four directions of the earth to offer their blessings, the audience turned with them in unison. Spiritual leaders blew smoke to the north, east, south, and west before turning back to the north to conclude that part of the blessing ceremony. Sharing Cahuilla Bird Songs and Serrano Mountain Sheep Songs, the singers illustrated that ancient song complexes still live in the Native American communities of Southern California. At the conclusion of the ceremony, participants mingled and partook of food and conversation before the hard work of filming began.

    Tlingit and Koyukon-Athabascan actor Martin Sensmeier played Willie Boy in Jason Momoa's *The Last Manhunt*. Born in Anchorage, Alaska, in 1985, the former oil worker has been a model and actor, playing in *The Magnificent Seven*, *Westworld,* and *Wind River* among other films. Martin's star is rising with a major role in the new film about Willie Boy. Mainei Kinimaka, a Native Hawai'ian from Kauai, joins Martin in *The Last Manhunt* as Carlota, the daughter of William and Maria Mike. Born in Kauai in 1988, Mainei and her sister, Maluia Kinimaka, are world class surfers and have worked diligently in the film industry. The lead roles also include Lakota actor Zahn McClarnon, with many films to his credit. Most recently he played Police Chief Mathias in the exciting *Longmire* series and had a part in *Westworld.* Zahn performed the role of William Mike, Carlota's father and the man murdered by Willie Boy on September 26, 1909. Finally, Blackfeet and Nez Perce actress Lily Gladstone undertook the role of Maria Mike, wife of William Mike and mother of

Carlota. Several others had roles in the film, including Jason Momoa who played Big Jim.

In addition to the professional actors, Momoa and Camarro secured the expertise of *Nuwuvi* singers and dancers to portray Chemehuevi culture accurately. Under the guidance of Matthew Leivas, approximately thirty men and women sang and danced as part of the movie. Their work will be presented in scenes representing the wakes of William Mike and Carlota Mike as well as the Ghost Dance sequence. Momoa and Camarro wanted audiences to hear three authentic songs, including Salt Songs and a Ghost Dance Song. The Salt Song Singers did not perform a *Yagapi* Ceremony, but they presented two authentic songs. In 1909, the Mike family held their wakes at the Serrano Big House on the Morongo Indian Reservation. In the film, the Salt Song Singers from the Chemehuevi and Colorado River Reservations sang for the souls of William and Carlota to *Nuva Kiav*, the hole in the sky where souls enter the afterlife. In addition to the two Salt Songs, the same men and women sang and danced an authentic Ghost Dance Song.

Guided by Leivas and the Chemehuevi singers, the group sang a *Nuwuvi* Ghost Dance Song, lending authenticity to the film. Tribal singers brought the song to life for the film, and they danced the Circle Dance, a derivative of the Ghost Dance, which remains a part of Chemehuevi culture today. Rather than using a song hastily composed for the movie, they performed an authentic Ghost Dance Song first sung in the nineteenth century but still sung today by Chemehuevi and Hualapai people. Leivas explained that he did not want the film depicting Ghost Dance songs from other tribes in the American West, but rather offered an authentic Ghost Dance Song known to his people, a song Willie Boy likely heard while participating in the solemn ceremony. The song chosen was one well known to tribal elders. In fact, in the 1990s, Chemehuevi elder Adrian Fisher told historians Sandos and Burgess that the Chemehuevi living on the Colorado River Indian and Chemehuevi Indian Reservations still sang Ghost Dance Songs. To provide an accurate depiction of the Ghost Dance Ceremony that Willie Boy had attended in his youth, Chemehuevi men and women donned white clay on their faces and hands as they danced the Ghost Dance for the camera. This reenactment provided an amazing scene, the most accurate portrayal of the Ghost Dance witnessed on film.

Chemehuevi from the Twenty-Nine Palms Tribe also participated in the making of *The Last Manhunt.* Two of the sons of Darrell and Corina Mike had parts in the movie, including nine-year-old Darrell James Mike II and six-year-old James Dean Mike. The boys acted as small children who engaged Willie Boy and Indian Agent Clara True. Three other tribal members also participated in the film. Angela Jane Mike, a long-time member of the Twenty-Nine Palms Tribal Council, and her two sons, Xol Antonius Nunez-Mike and Cruz Guillaume Nunez-Mike, joined in the film. Members of the Mike family, all descendants of William and Maria Mike, added greater authenticity, even as they experienced the long hours necessary to set up scenes, rehearse their parts, and shoot scenes several times. Filming occurred out of doors in Palm Canyon on the Agua Caliente Indian Reservation in Palm Springs, California. Momoa and Camargo shot the movie on several locations in Southern California on or near where the historical events transpired, not in a movie studio. The filming of *The Last Manhunt* utilized various landscapes key to the historical account of Willie Boy, both in the Colorado

Desert and the Mojave Desert of Southern California, which also lends reality to this film.

The Last Manhunt successfully captured the depth of feeling between two young people who truly loved each other but were caught up in the cultural tension between traditional Chemehuevi beliefs and the modern era of the early twentieth century Native America. As Mary Lou Brown explained, "love is hard." For Willie Boy, Carlota, William, and the Mike family, the love between two young people caused great trauma and hardship that is still felt by Chemehuevi and other Southern Paiute people. For *Nuwuvi* people, the relationship between Willie Boy and Carlota Mike was forbidden by tribal law and tradition. The film captures the couple's deep feelings for each other and their desire to be together, in spite of tribal conventions. Following the accidental shooting of Mr. Mike, Willie Boy and Carlota fled into the expansive ocean of rock and sand. They ran into the light and shadows of the Mojave Desert to meet their fates.

Willie Boy and Carlota met tragic ends in the mountains of the Mojave Desert, the place of their birth and early lives. Their story is intimately tied to the rugged landscape known as the Mojave Desert where Chemehuevi people still relate to the plants, animals, and sites of power. Their story is still remembered at the Oasis of Mara, the present-day home of the 29 Palms Inn near Joshua Tree National Park. Willie Boy and Carlota had intimate knowledge of their place on earth, and this same place continues to hold the story of a love gone wrong and the untimely deaths of a father, daughter and grandmother. The Mojave Desert is the remembered earth that holds truth about the Chemehuevi couple and their families. The places are remembered each time the Salt Songs are sung at wakes, when singers bring forward and make alive again the ancient accounts of sites along the Salt Song Trail. William and Carlota Mike died suddenly and violently. Mrs. Ticup died from being shaken and broken hearted. Willie Boy contracted an evil wind that entered his lungs, admitting bacteria that consumed his lungs – some say the consequence of his evil acts.

    Willie Boy died a long and painful death from consumption. Southern Paiute secreted his body in an unmarked grave in the shadow of his creation mountain. They wanted no one to disturb the remains of the Chemehuevi runner. Yet, the spirit of Willie Boy and his love for Carlota has never died. Throughout Indian Country, Willie Boy's spirit lives on in legend and story. Indians people far and wide know Willie Boy's story and share that narrative to anyone who will listen. Cahuilla Bird Singers even created the Willie Boy Song, which they share to the delight of indigenous audiences. Chemehuevi, Southern Paiute, and other Indians of the Great Basin and Southwest tell versions of Willie Boy's story. Native Americans will tell you simply: "The posse never got Willie Boy. He got away." Willie Boy lives today as an iconic figure of the American West. He is a symbol of the enduring American Indian spirit, liberty, and freedom, emblematic of Native American independence and sovereignty.

Bibliography

Archival Collections

Colorado River Indian Tribes Library and Museum, Parker, Arizona.

Costo Library, University of California, Riverside.

Executive Order, President Grover Cleveland, November 11, 1895, "The United States of America To All To Whom These Presents Shall Come." Copy in the Tribal Library, Twenty-Nine Palms Tribe, Coachella, California.

Gerald Smith Collection. Archives, A.K. Smiley Library, Redlands, California.

Gillman Ranch, Riverside County Park, Banning, California.

Harvey Johnson Collection, Arizona Historical Society, Yuma, Arizona.

John P. Harrington. National Anthropological Archives, Smithsonian Institution, Washington, D.C. Microfilm copy, Rivera Library, University of California, Riverside.

Matthew Hanks Leivas Collection, Chemehuevi Indian Reservation.

Matthew Hanks Leivas Family Records.

Maud Carrico Russell Manuscript and Collection, Old Schoolhouse, Twentynine Palms Historical Society.

Office of Indian Affairs, Records of the Mission Agency, Record Group 75, National Archives, Pacific Southwest Region.

Papers of John P. Harrington, Smithsonian Institution, Washington, D.C., Copies in the Rivera Library, University of California, Riverside.

Paul Smith Collection, 29 Palms Inn, Twentynine Palms, California.

Records of the Bureau of Indian Affairs, Record Group 75, National Archives, Pacific Southwest Region, Perris, California.

Special Collections, University of California, Riverside.

Twentynine Palms City Library, Twentynine Palms, California.

Twentynine Palms Historical Society, Twentynine Palms, California.

Twenty-Nine Palms Indian Tribe Archives, Coachella, California.

Twenty-Nine Palms Band files, Bureau of Indian Affairs, Southern California Agency, Riverside, California.

Original Sources

Benítez, Joseph Mike. Testimony of Joe Benitez presented at the Willie Boy Symposium, Riverside County Historical Society. Gilman Ranch Museum, Banning, California. September 26, 2009.

Censuses of 1910, Typescript, Twenty-Nine Palms Band of Mission Indians Library, Coachella, California.

Census of the Twenty-Nine Palms Band, 1890, Mission Indian Agency, National Archives, Record Group 75, Microfilm 595, Roll 257.

Census of the Twenty-Nine Palms Band, 1892, Mission Indian Agency, National Archives, Microfilm 595, Roll 257.

Census of the Twenty-Nine Palms Band, 1894-1897, Mission Indian Agency, National Archives, Microfilm 595, Roll 258.

Email Communication. Joseph Mike Benitez to Clifford E. Trafzer, June 5, 2001. Author's Collection.

Ives, Joseph Christmas. *"Report Upon the Colorado River of the West."* Report of the Secretary of War, 1861, in Senate Executive Document, 36th Congress, 1st Session. Washington, D.C.: Government Printing Office, 1861.

Leivas, Matthew and Kurt Russo, "Ways of Knowing Landscapes: Representations of Sacred Landscapes." Unpublished Manuscript provided by the authors.

Sauvel, Katherine Siva and Eric Elliott, *'Isill Héqwas Wåaxish: A Dried Coyote's Tail*, 2 Volumes. Banning, California: Malki Museum Press, 2004.

Stoffle, Richard W., Richard Arnold, and Kathleen Van Vlack, "Facing the Unimaginable: Hopi and Southern Paiutes Respond to Massive Risk Events," May 14, 2013, Unpublished Manuscript provided by Richard W. Stoffle.

"Summary Testimony by Richard Arnold in Response, Hidden Hills Generating System," February 4, 2013, provided by Matthew Hanks Leivas.

"The Enugwuhype (Ancestral Numic People): An Ethnogenesis Analysis." Unpublished manuscript provided by Richard W. Stoffle to the author.

Trafzer Journal, Field Notes, 2001-7.

Oral Histories

Anonymous Paiute. Interview by Clifford E. Trafzer. Spring Mountains, Nevada, October 6, 2012.

Anderson, Kenneth. Interview by Clifford E. Trafzer. Las Vegas Paiute Indian Reservation, July 10-11, 2006.

Bean, Lowell. Interview by Clifford E. Trafzer. Telephone interview. March 1, 2012.

Benitez, Joe. Interview by James Sandos and Larry E. Burgess. August 12, 1989. In James Sandos and Larry Burgess. *The Hunt for Willie Boy: Indian-Hating and Popular Culture.* Norman: University of Oklahoma Press, 1994.

———. Interview by Clifford E. Trafzer. Twenty- Nine Palms Indian Reservation, September 10, 17, 1997.

———. Interview by Clifford E. Trafzer. Cabazon Indian Reservation, September 29, 2000.

———. Internet communication with Clifford E. Trafzer. June 5, 2001.

———. Interview by Clifford E. Trafzer. September 14, 2001.

———. Interview by Clifford E. Trafzer. Cabazon Indian Reservation, November 30, 2001.

Brown, Mary Lou. Interview by James Sandos and Larry E. Burgess. February 1 and 15, 1991. In James Sandos and Larry Burgess. *The Hunt for Willie Boy: Indian-Hating and Popular Culture.* Norman: University of Oklahoma Press, 1994.

Burgess, Larry. Interview by Clifford E. Trafzer. Telephone interview. September 18, 2001.

———. Interview by Clifford E. Trafzer. Redlands, California. August 29, 2013.

Chief Pancoyer, Chemehuevi. Oral interview by Agent J. L. Stanley, in the Coachella Valley in Stanley to Dent, Records of the Arizona Superintendent of Indian Affairs, National Archives, Microfilm 734, Reel 2.

Cornelius, Betty. Interview by Clifford E. Trafzer. Colorado River Indian Reservation, January 10, 2013.

Davis, Jason. Interview by Clifford E. Trafzer. University of California, Riverside, February 2013.

De Crevecoeur, Ben. Interview by Maud Russell. Russell Manuscript.

Earl, David. Paper given at California Indian Conference, Chaffey College, Rancho Cucamonga, California.

Eddy, Larry. Interview by Clifford E. Trafzer. California State University, San Bernardino, September 28, 2001.

____. Interview by Clifford E. Trafzer. Colorado River Indian Reservation, October 18, 2007.

Johnson, Harvey. Interview by Clifford E. Trafzer. Yuma, Arizona. June 1973.

Leivas, Ace and Matthew. Interview by Clifford E. Trafzer, August 29, 2013, Riverside, California.

Leivas, Gertrude. Interview by Clifford E. Trafzer, Theresa Mike, Matthew Leivas, Anthony Madrigal and Bernie Thomas. Chemehuevi Indian Reservation, March 1999.

Leivas, Iris and Matthew. Interview by Clifford E. Trafzer. Chemehuevi Indian Reservation, February 17-19, 2013.

Leivas, Jake, Vivienne, and Matthew. Public Presentation of Salt Songs. Twentynine Palms, California, March 1999.

Leivas, Matthew. Interview by Clifford E. Trafzer. Palm Desert, California, August 4, 2013.

———. Interview by Clifford E. Trafzer. Telephone interview. October 15, 1997.

———. Interview by Clifford E. Trafzer. Chemehuevi Indian Reservation, September 5, 2000.

———. Interview by Clifford E. Trafzer. Twenty-Nine Palms Reservation, September 12, 2000.

———. Interview by Clifford E. Trafzer. Telephone interview. May 16, 2001.

———. Interview by Clifford E. Trafzer. September 27, 2001.

———. Interview by Clifford E. Trafzer. Chemehuevi Indian Reservation, April 8, 2002.

———. Interview by Clifford E. Trafzer. Chemehuevi Indian Reservation, December 5, 2005.

———. Interview by Clifford E. Trafzer. Hawaiiyo, East of the Chemehuevi Indian Reservation, 2010, as found in Clifford E. Trafzer, Keeping the Songs Alive, DVD, 2010.

———. Interview by Clifford E. Trafzer. Chemehuevi Indian Reservation, November 27, 2011.

———. Interview by Clifford E. Trafzer. Chemehuevi Indian Reservation, October 5, 2012.

———. Interview by Clifford E. Trafzer. Telephone interview. June 15, 2013.

———. Interview by Clifford E. Trafzer, Twenty-Nine Palms Reservation July 23, 2013.

Mahone, Keith. Interview by Clifford E. Trafzer. Twenty-Nine Palms Indian Reservation, November 1997.

———. Interview by Clifford E. Trafzer. Chemehuevi Indian Reservation, August 31, 2019.

Mathes, Valerie. Interview by Clifford E. Trafzer. Telephone interview. September 29- 30, 2001.

Mike, Dean. Interview by Clifford E. Trafzer. Twenty-Nine Palms Indian Reservation, September 2-3, 1997.

———. Interview by Clifford E. Trafzer. Twenty-Nine Palms Indian Reservation, October 24, 1997.

———. Interview by Clifford E. Trafzer. Twenty-Nine Palms Indian Reservation, September 10, 2001.

———. Interview by Clifford E. Trafzer. Twenty-Nine Palms Indian Reservation, August 4, 2013.

———. Interview by Clifford E. Trafzer. Twenty-Nine Palms Indian Reservation, August 8, 2013.

Mike, Jennifer. Interview by Anthony Madrigal. Twenty-Nine Palms Reservation. March 2-3, 2000.

Mike, Jennifer Estama. Interview by Clifford E. Trafzer. Twenty-Nine Palms Reservation, January 28, 2002.

Mike, Theresa. Interview by Clifford E. Trafzer. Twenty-Nine Palms Reservation, November 15, 1997.

———. Interview by Clifford E. Trafzer. Twenty-Nine Palms Reservation, March 1, 2001.

———. Interview by Clifford E. Trafzer. Telephone interview. August 31, 2005.

Mitre, Alfreda. Interview by Clifford E. Trafzer. Las Vegas Paiute Indian Reservation, July 10-11, 2006.

Morongo, Nellie. Oral history notes by Maud Russell. Twenty-Nine Palms Historical Society, circa 1940.

Murillo, Pauline Ormego. Interview by Clifford E. Trafzer. San Manuel Indian Reservation, March 2000.

———. Interview by Clifford E. Trafzer. Telephone interview. May 8, 2001.

———. Interview by Clifford E. Trafzer. San Manuel Indian Reservation, May 15, 2001. Pakuuma. Interview by John Harrington. Harrington Papers, 1915.

Park ranger. Interview by Clifford E. Trafzer. Gilman Ranch, Riverside County Park, Banning, California. June, 2000.

Russo, Kurt. Email communication with Clifford E. Trafzer, August 29, 2005.

———. Interview by Clifford E. Trafzer. Cabazon and Twenty-Nine Palms Reservation, Coachella, California, May 7, 2006.

Saubel, Katherine. Interview by Clifford E. Trafzer. Southwest Airlines Flight, Sacramento to Ontario, California, and Morongo Indian Reservation. September 15, 2000.

———. Interview by Clifford E. Trafzer. Telephone interview. May 8, 2001.

Smith, Paul. Interview with Clifford E. Trafzer. 29 Palms Inn, March 3, 2000.

Smith, Paul and Jane. Interview by Clifford E. Trafzer. Twentynine Palms, California, June 1999.

———. Interview by Clifford E. Trafzer. Twentynine Palms, California. May 7, 2001.

Unidentified elder. Interview by Gerald Smith. Smith Collection, Smiley Library.

Van Fleet, Alberta. Interview by James Sandos and Larry E. Burgess. January 5 and February 15, 1991. In James Sandos and Larry Burgess. *The Hunt for Willie Boy: Indian-Hating and Popular Culture.* Norman: University of Oklahoma Press, 1994.

Vaughn, Ted. Interview with Clifford E. Trafzer. Yavapai-Prescott Indian Reservation, November 6, 2008 and January 8, 2009.

Newspapers

Arizona Citizen
Arizona Sentinel
Banning Record
Daily Alta California
Desert Trails
Los Angeles Daily Times
Los Angeles Herald
Lost Angeles Herald Examiner
Los Angeles Record
Los Angeles Star
New York Times
Redlands Daily Facts
Redlands Daily Review
Riverside Morning Mission
San Bernardino Sun
San Diego Herald
Seattle Star

Books and Articles

Bean, Lowell J., ed. *California Indian Shamanism*. Menlo Park, California: Ballena Press, 1992.

____, and Lisa J. Bourgeault, *The Cahuilla*. New York: Chelsea House Publishers, 1989.

____, and Katherine Siva Saubel. T*emalpakh: Cahuilla Indian Knowledge and Usage of Plants.* Banning, California: Malki Museum Press, 1972.

Carling, James L. "On the Trail of Willie Boy." *Desert Magazine* (November 1946): 6.

Culp, Georgia Laird. "The Chemehuevis." *Desert Magazine* (March 1975): 18-21, 38.

Edwards, Harold L. "Willie Boy and the Posse." *The Californians* (November-December 1989): 48-54.

Erickson, Zoe. *Caught Dead to Rights: The Biography of Ben de Crevecoeur, A Real Western Lawman.* CreateSpace, 2009.

Euler, Robert C. *The Paiute People.* Phoenix: Indian Tribal Series, 1972.

____. *Southern Paiute Ethnography.* Salt Lake City: Anthropological Papers, University of Utah Press, 1966.

Fowler, Catherine S. "Reconstructing Southern Paiute-Chemehuevi Trails in the Mojave Desert of Southern Nevada and California: Ethnographic Perspectives from the 1930s." In James Snead, Clark Erickson, and J. Andrew Darling, eds., *Landscapes of Movement: Trails, Paths, and Roads in Anthropological Perspective*, Philadelphia: University of Pennsylvania Museum of Archaeology and Anthropology, 2009.

Fowler, Don D. and Catherine S., eds., "Anthropology of the Numa: John Wesley Powell's Manuscripts on the Numic Peoples of Western North America, 1868-1880." Smithsonian Institution, *Contributions to Anthropology* 14 (Washington, D.C.: 1971).

Gayton, A. H. "The Ghost Dance of 1870 in South-Central California." In *University of California Publications in American Archaeology and Ethnology* 28 (1930-31): 57-82.

Hanks, Richard A. *This War is for a Whole Life: The Culture of Resistance Among Southern California Indians, 1850-1966.* Banning, California: Dorothy Ramon Learning Center, Ushkana Press, 2012.

Heizer, Robert F., ed. *Handbook of North American Indians*: *California.* Washington, D.C.: Smithsonian Institution Press, 1978.

Hittman, Michael. *Wovoka and the Ghost Dance.* Yerington, Nevada: Yerington Paiute Tribe, 1990.

Hughes, Tom. *History of Banning and San Gorgonio Pass.* Banning, California: Banning Record Print, 1939.

Johnson, Captain W. R., Manuscript. In Robert C. Euler, *Southern Paiute Ethnography.* Salt Lake City: Anthropological Papers, University of Utah Press, 1966.

Kelly, Isabel. "Southern Paiute Ethnography." *Glen Canyon Series 21.* University of Utah Anthropological Papers 69. Salt Lake City, 1964.

Kelly, Isabel. *Southern Paiute Ethnohistory.* New York: Garland Publishing, 1976.

King, Chester and Dennis Casebier. *Background to Historic and Prehistoric Resources of the East Mojave Desert Region.* Riverside, California: United States Department of Interior, Bureau of Land Management, 1981.

Knack, Martha C. *Boundaries Between: the Southern Paiutes, 1775-1995.* Lincoln: University of Nebraska Press, 2001.

Kroeber, Alfred. *Handbook of the Indians of California.* Berkeley: University of California Press, 1953.

Laird, Carobeth. *The Chemehuevis.* Banning, California: Malki Museum Press, 1976.

_____. "Chemehuevi Religious Beliefs and Practices," *The Journal of California Anthropology* 1 (Spring, 1974): 19-25.

———. "Chemehuevi Religious Beliefs and Practices," AVAS Newsletter, March 1982, in Gerald A. Smith Collection, Smiley Library, Redlands, California.

———. "Chemehuevi Shamanism, Sorcery, and Charms," *Journal of California and Great Basin Anthropology* 2 (1980): 80-87.

Lawton, Harry. *Willie Boy: A Western Manhunt.* Balboa Island, California: Paisano Press, 1960.

Leivas, Matthew. "Chemehuevi: Nuwu Who-vee-up." Unpublished song by Leivas. Author's Collection.

Martineau, LaVan. *Southern Paiutes: Legends, Lore, Language, and Lineage.* Las Vegas: K.C. Publications, 1992.

Mooney, James. *The Ghost-Dance Religion and Wounded Knee.* New York: Dover Publications, Reprint, 1973.

Moses, L. G. "The Father Tells Me So! Wovoka: The Ghost Dance Prophet." In *American Indian Quarterly* 9 (1985): 335-51.

Phillips, George H. *Chiefs and Challengers: Indian Resistance and Cooperation in Southern California.* Berkeley: University of California Press, 1975.

Ramon, Dorothy and Eric Elliot. *Wayta' Yawa': Always Believe.* Banning, California: Malki Museum Press, 2000.

Russell, Maud Carrico. "Early Days at Twenty-Nine Palms," *Desert Spotlight*, February 1948, Vertical Files, Twenty-Nine Palms Library.

____. "Indian Reservations at Twenty-Nine Palms." Russell Collection, Twenty-Nine Palms Historical Society.

____. "Old Indian Burial Grounds." *Desert Spotlight*, Vertical Files, Twentynine Palms City Library, Twentynine Palms, California.

____. "Pioneer Days." *Desert Spotlight*, Vertical Files, Twentynine Palms City Library, Twentynine Palms, California.

Sandos, James, and Larry Burgess. *The Hunt for Willie Boy: Indian-Hating and Popular Culture*. Norman: University of Oklahoma Press, 1994.

Sauvel, Katherine Siva, and Eric Elliott. *Isill Heqwas Waaxish*, Volume 1. Banning, California: Malki Museum Press, 2004.

Scott, Lalla. Karnee: *A Paiute Narrative*. Reno: University of Nevada Press, 1966.

Seiler, Hansjakob. "Willie Boy: A Western Drama." *The Indian Historian* 1 (1968): 26-27. This article contains an account from Chona Dominquez, Cahuilla, Torres-Martinez Indian Reservation. She claimed that Willie Boy's Native name was Meyhayus.

Smoak, Gregory E. *Ghost Dances and Identity: Prophetic Religion and American Indian Ethnogenesis in the Nineteenth Century.* Berkeley: University of California Press, 2006.

Trafzer, Clifford E. *A Chemehuevi Song: Resilience of a Southern California Tribe.* Seattle: University of Washington Press, 2016.

____. *As Long as the Grass Shall Grow and Rivers Flow: A History of Native Americans.* Belmont, California: Wadsworth, 2000.

____. "Chemehuevi Indian Creation." In Ruth Nolan, ed., *No Place for a Puritan: The Literature of California's Deserts,* Berkeley: Heyday Books, 2009.

____. *Chemehuevi Indians: Historic Properties of Traditional Lands on the Yuma Proving Ground.* Riverside: University of California, Riverside. California Center for Native Nations, 2013.

____. *Historic Property Inventory, Traditional Cultural Properties: Yavapai-Prescott Cultural Ethnography of Lands on the Yuma Proving Ground.* Riverside: University of California, Riverside. California Center for Native Nations, 2010.

____. "Invisible Enemies: Ranching, Farming, and Quechan Indian Deaths at the Fort Yuma Agency, California, 1915-1925." *American Indian Culture and Research Journal* 21 (1997): 83-117.

____. "Medical Circles Defeating Tuberculosis in Southern California." *Canadian Bulletin of Medical History* 23 (2006): 477-498.

____. *Mojave of the Colorado River Indian Reservation: Historic Property Inventory Traditional Cultural Properties: Mojave of the Colorado River Indian Reservation Cultural Ethnography of the Lands on the Yuma Proving Ground.* Riverside: University of California, Riverside. California Center for Native Nations, 2011.

____. *Quechan Indian Historic Properties of Traditional Lands on the Yuma Proving Ground.* Riverside: University of California, Riverside. California Center for Native Nations, 2012.

____. *The People of San Manuel.* Highland, California: San Manuel Band of Mission Indians, 2002.

____. "Tuberculosis Death and Survival Among Southern California Indians, 1922-1944." *Canadian Bulletin of Medical History* 18 (2000): 85-107.

____. Yuma: *Frontier Crossing of the Far Southwest.* Wichita, Kansas: Western Heritage Press, 1980.

____. Luke Madrigal, and Anthony Madrigal. *Chemehuevi People of the Coachella Valley.* Coachella, California: Chemehuevi Press of the Twenty-Nine Palms Tribe, 1997.

____. and Joel R. Hyer, eds. *Exterminate Them! Written Accounts of the Murder, Rape, and Enslavement of Native*

Americans during the California Gold Rush. East Lansing: Michigan State University Press, 1999.

True, Clara. "The Willie Boy Case and Attendant Circumstances," Office of Indian Affairs, file number 79987-09, published by Harry Lawton in *The Journal of California Anthropology* 5 (Summer, 1978): 115-123.

Van Valkenburgh, Richard F., "Chemehuevi Notes." In Isabel T. Kelly, *Southern Paiute Ethnography*. New York: Garland Publishing, 1976.

Wood, Willard S. "Bad Indian in the Morongos." *Westways* (April, 1935): 10-11.

www.ingramcontent.com/pod-product-compliance
Lightning Source LLC
LaVergne TN
LVHW051042080426
835508LV00019B/1666